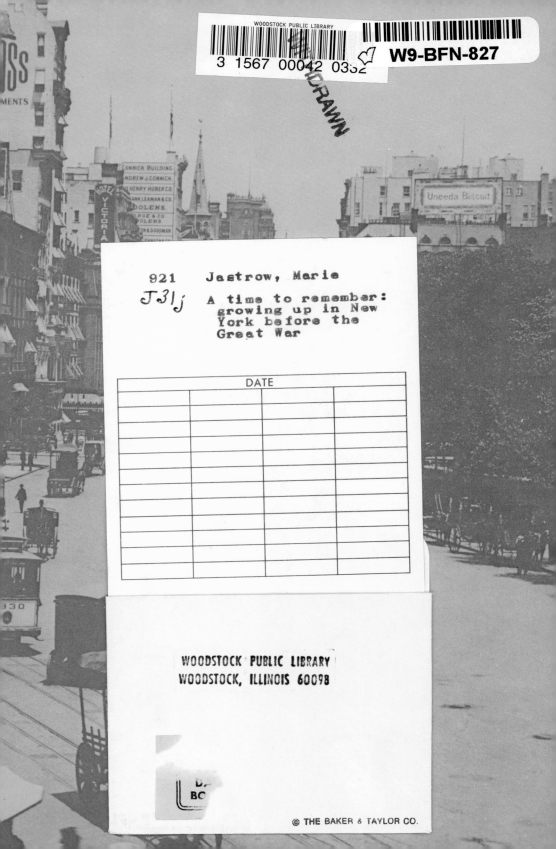

921
J31j

Jastrow, Marie

A time to remember: growing up in New York before the Great War

DATE			

© THE BAKER & TAYLOR CO.

A Time to Remember

A Time to Remember

Growing Up In New York Before The Great War

Marie Jastrow

W.W. NORTON & COMPANY, INC.

NEW YORK · LONDON

To the memory of my parents

Contents

A Time to Remember

Introduction

THIS IS A STORY of an early America. It is the story of an immigrant girl growing up in New York at the turn of the century.

Our life was an ordinary life; there were no glittering adventures in it; my father never became a rich man. I have no glorious, remarkable story to tell, beyond the glorious and remarkable story of the millions who migrated to a new land and settled there. Adventurers, dreamers, scholars, beggars—they came during a time when the gates of America were open to the world. These gates were never open as wide again. It was a unique moment in history.

By the beginning of the century, the tempo of immigration from Europe had increased to the point where every day thousands of immigrants passed through Ellis Island in New York Harbor. Once an immigrant passed the rigid health inspection and was permitted to land, he was on his own, free to go where he wished. A few daring souls scattered throughout the United States, but most of the newcomers stayed on in New York. To the immigrant, New York *was* America. In his mind, the two merged into one image of the goals he had set for himself and his children. He had braved the ocean, he had survived the steerage horrors in the bowels of the ship, he had landed in America; he could go no further. New York was his haven.

But the contrast between the promise and the reality was often devastating. For most immigrants, life in New York was a bitter struggle. No one had money; most of us lived on the most meager of earnings. But no one felt deprived. No one felt trapped. No one measured his life except in dogged perseverance, purpose and hope. For mettle and backbone those early immigrants, who endured the steerage crossing to pursue their dream of America, had no equal. Out of their old world needs, the new world was born.

Who could feel poor, who could feel deprived, when his future lay in the heart of such an America—when his child could go to college, when he could end up a doctor, a lawyer, a judge of the Supreme Court? Who knew? In America a man could be anything he wished.

1

Papa Came Steerage

MY FATHER WAS BORN IN 1869 in a small province of Austria, the youngest of four brothers. He was about five years old when his family moved to a small town in Serbia near Yarac, where my father would meet and marry my mother some thirty years later.

When my father was thirteen, after his Bar Mitzvah, his future came into discussion. "My boy," he was told, "now that you're a man, you must learn some business so you can make your own way in the world." The family could no longer provide for him, his father said. To my father's dismay, the stark reality of sudden manhood brought him to an apprenticeship in a flour mill. His future in the business world thus assured, the youngest son was packed off to live at the mill.

But the family had not fully reckoned with their son, who soon discovered that he did not at all have a flour-mill temperament. My father stood it as long as he could, and then solved the problem in the only way he knew. He ran away. He gathered his few belongings, flung the bundle across his shoulder, and took off.

Papa was always rather vague about how he managed to survive after that, perhaps because he didn't want to remember those years. I do remember his telling me that several years later he landed in a bookshop in Zurich, where he found work as a clerk. The family who ran the establishment liked and befriended him. As I recall, Papa said that he was taken into their home as a son. He stayed there about ten years. Those must have been happy years, because my father talked of his benefactors with love and affection, although he never made it quite clear why he left them.

At any rate, the years in the Zurich bookshop must have given him some polish, because, when he finally did go back to his Serbian home town for a visit, he was considered a great match for the available daughters.

A few months later, on May 12, 1898, my mother, at the age of seventeen, became the bride of Julius Grunfeld. My father was thirty.

According to Mama, her dowry was quite substantial. Her family, the Deutsches, clearly believed that their daughter had married a paragon of all the virtues, worthy of a generous marriage settlement.

Now everyone came forward with advice. Papa's brothers, all successful businessmen, felt a sense of "noblesse oblige." The oldest brother was in the textile business. With part of the dowry and his brother's help, my father established himself in a dry goods and textile store in a bustling little town near Yarac. But what no one knew then was that my father had not the slightest talent for business.

So there was my father, totally unprepared, confronted with the formidable task of running a dry goods store. From the beginning it was a struggle. Naivete and a lack of business judgment became apparent. The store began to lose money. Unfortunately, Papa did not have the faintest idea what remedies the situation required. He said he needed time—time to learn, time to set things to rights. So he held on. With stubborn determination he managed to carry the shaky enterprise into its third year.

Sometime in February 1902, after a difficult winter season, Papa said, he was forced to close his doors. It was one of the most unhappy periods in his life.

I was then three. With a wife and child to support, Papa was in no position to argue when Mama's father prevailed upon him to open a general merchandising store in the neighboring town of Brod. "There was no risk," my grandfather said; "the town needed a store of that kind."

Surprisingly, everything went well, and the business prospered. On the first anniversary, everything was still going splendidly. Papa was now confident that he could succeed and redeem himself. The family breathed easier; their choice of a son-in-law had been a wise one after all. And then the roof fell in. Another store opened nearby. The new store offered cheaper merchandise, and Papa's customers began to fall away. When the situation became desperate, my grandfather urged him to lower his standards and meet the competition head-on. "Never," said my father. "Never would he sell shoddy merchandise."

Well, the new year of 1905 had barely begun when the inevitable happened. Papa lost his business. Another failure.

Meanwhile, word of the new land across the ocean was spreading through Europe like wildfire. America was on every tongue. And talk of the "Golden Land" eventually reached Brod, that remote corner of Serbia where my parents lived.

Suddenly, to save his pride, my father announced that he was going to America. In America lay his future, he said. People had been known to make their fortunes there. One only needed the courage to break away.

Mama told him he was insane. Never would she leave her homeland. But my father, always the adventurer, could not be dissuaded. He was going to America.

The plan was for us to stay with my mother's people, the Deutsches, at their home in Yarac while we awaited the outcome of Papa's American venture. His ship, a Hamburg-American liner, was due to sail toward the end of September, in 1905.

And so we came to the lovely Serbian town of Yarac on the Sava River, my mother's girlhood home.

It was a large, sprawling, tree-shaded house that Mama grew up in. And what a contrast to the tenement

16

walk-ups that would be her homes in America. My father did his best, but all his days, here in New York, he remained a working man. He found, as did so many thousands who came before and after him, that in golden America, money did not grow on trees.

My recollections of our stay in Yarac stand out clearly. I remember vast fields of grain swaying in waves of gold with the gentle Adriatic breezes. I remember cows being milked by the servants. Totally wonderful to my child's fancy was a deep subcellar that kept marvelous foods fresh—shelves of jars filled with fruit, and freshly churned butter, and milk from which the heavy, yellow top was skimmed off for the "schlagsahne" or whipped cream. Coffee, and almost everything that was baked, was covered with that wonderful whipped cream.

By far the busiest person in the house was my tiny, dark-eyed grandmother, in her grey silk dress with cream-colored lace, giving orders to the household. And there was Mama's younger sister, sixteen, excitedly awaiting the holidays that heralded young gentlemen callers. How I loved the hustle and bustle of the holiday preparations, the tremendous excitement in the house, with relatives arriving from far-away villages for the holidays. For one whole week, the big, sunny kitchen was astir with activity. Huge pots steamed on the stove. Everybody was busy with something. I was shunted from one end of the kitchen to the other, always underfoot, but staying around, holding myself in readiness for any little goody that might come my way. I especially liked cleaning the jam and whipped-cream pans after they had been emptied.

At mealtimes, the big table in the dining room groaned under the weight of wonderful food that had been prepared for the aunts and uncles and cousins. About a dozen children were seated separately around a smaller table. For dessert, there were cakes and those marvelous little plum and apricot tarts that my own mother baked so often later, when I was growing up in New York. They were spicy, bite-sized, melt-in-your-mouth, good things to eat.

And most of all, woven through that picture, I see my grandfather's authoritative, calming influence, as he walked about smoking his long-stemmed, aromatic pipe. Mama's father was the direct antithesis to Papa, who was more the intellectual. Grandfather was a doer, a dynamic personality. Unlike the other older men, he did not wear a beard. Many years later, his photograph still showed a clean-shaven face.

My grandfather was a superb horseman. When horse and rider galloped through those massive gates that were thrown wide open by the coachman, that was something to see. Grandfather owned only high-spirited Arabians, Mama said. He was afraid of nothing. He kept two huge, ferocious dogs that were chained during the day, but released after sundown, when the heavy gates were closed and locked against marauders. No one dared go into that yard after sundown unless he was well acquainted with those dogs.

My mother's parents in Yarac, Serbia, around 1900.

PAPA CAME STEERAGE

As I write this, almost three-quarters of a century later, and remember my mother's parents, I cherish the few years that I was allowed to know them. They were a grand old pair, my grandparents.

But suddenly, with a rude shock, my mind is brought away from that long-ago time, as I realize that I am no longer the little girl of six who romped happily in my grandparents' home. In fact, I am now much older than my grandparents were when I knew them. And I am filled with helpless amazement.

Well, time did not stand still for my father as it did for me in my mind. The last week in September had come and gone and the waiting was over. Papa was bound for America.

2

A Moment of Panic

MY FATHER CROSSED THE ATLANTIC and landed on Ellis Island at the beginning of October 1905, well aware of the ordeal that awaited him. He had heard stories. The threat of deportation haunted every immigrant; at least every steerage immigrant.

Eyes, ears, chest—the entire person was scrutinized by doctors. Some were rejected. Those who were turned away fell into the depths of despair, waiting, without hope, for the first ship to take them back.

Hour after hour the examination went on. At last my father found himself on American soil, a silent, solitary figure. He had passed the inspection. Now, for the first time, he was alone, separated from his fellow travellers. It was a painful aloneness. During the two weeks of his stay on the ocean liner, his life had fallen into a daily rhythm, and now, suddenly there was nothing. Hopefully he glanced around, but no familiar face was in sight.

When an immigrant was alone, he was usually assisted by "helpers" or "conductors" who came from his part of the world, and spoke his language. If friends or relatives were waiting for him, he was welcomed with open arms. But no "helper" approached Papa, nor were there any friends or relatives to welcome him. He often said that he never felt as abandoned as he did on that day, his first in America.

"What to do?" His destiny had brought him safely thus far. Surely the gods would not desert him. But the truth was that Papa was near panic.

He sat down on a bench in Battery Park to consider his position. Shelter was his first need. A cheap hotel? But where? He decided to ask the first uniformed man he saw for advice.

Now and then people passed him. But they only glanced his way for an indifferent moment and walked briskly on. An afternoon wind began blowing in from the ocean. It had been a balmy October day, but a cold blast hit the Battery now; time to get on with it. He got up from the bench, rising slowly. Then, with a hopeless feeling he sat down again. How did one get around in a big city like New York? How, dear God, did one find a cheap hotel?

Another gust of the October wind chilled him to the marrow. He drew his coat closer. Later, Papa admitted that at that moment he was close to tears.

A policeman walked by and stopped. What was this lonely figure doing in the cold afternoon, sitting in the park? An immigrant, no doubt, just off the ship. My father looked up, saw this uniformed giant towering

22

over him, and a sudden fear struck his heart. A policeman! Policemen weren't exactly the best friends people had, where he came from. His one overpowering need was to get away fast. But to his dismay the officer held him back.

Where was he going? Had he lost the ticket with the address of his destination on it? My father breathed easier; the officer eyed him kindly. That was a thing unheard of in his memory of policemen. What language did he speak? German, said my father, who spoke several languages—French, Serbian. He selected German because it seemed universal.

"Are you expecting anyone?" The officer spoke some German. My father shook his head. No, he expected no one, he knew no one. But he would appreciate help in locating a room. "Can you pay?" "Yes," Papa again shook his head. "But not much." He hesitated a moment. "The room has to be cheap."

The policeman smiled, writing something on a slip of paper.

"Go to this address. Tell them that Officer Schmidt gave you this." My father looked at the address he had just received. His one dilemma, how to get through the streets of this impossible city, still paralyzed his brain. He wondered how to get to the address he was holding in his hand, but dared not ask.

Officer Schmidt was becoming impatient. "What is it? Can't you read?"

"Yes, I can read", said my father, "but, if you would

be so kind to give me directions, I do not know this city."

"Of course, you just got in," laughed the officer. "I'll take you to the streetcar on that corner. You give this address to the conductor, he will let you off in the right street."

"Thank you," said my grateful father. "I shall never forget this—how you helped me on my first day in America."

"That's all right. I could see you needed help. Good luck."

Then my father suddenly remembered that he had an uncle somewhere in New York, but he was certain his uncle was not expecting him. Yes, the address was in the notebook he had with him. But this uncle left for America many years ago, when he was about seventeen, and my father was a little boy. Perhaps it would be better if he were to forget about it after all. He had no wish to go to his relative as a beggar.

No, the officer thought that relatives should be contacted; "a man alone in the city needed all the help he could get." He looked at my father hard. "You sure he *is* your uncle, now?" My father nodded. "Yes, my mother's brother."

"Well, what are you hesitating for? A blood relative."

"But thirty years—thirty years ago he left. I was a child. I haven't seen him since."

"Come on, find the notebook with the man's address."

They found the address. It was a hotel on Fifty-seventh Street near Fifth Avenue. Still my father made no move to go anywhere but to the streetcar that would take him to Hester Street, and the address the officer had given him.

"Come on, man, your uncle will probably put you up tonight. After all you are his sister's son."

My father nodded his head. Whatever else the policeman said about his uncle, this made sense.

Yet, he hesitated. "Well, are you going?" Officer Schmidt was becoming impatient, he could not understand Papa's hesitation. Indeed, my father barely understood himself. In the end, he went. With the policeman's help he found his way to the elevated train, his first contact with transportation in the big city. He walked west on Fifty-seventh Street to his uncle's hotel.

What followed then was totally unexpected.

In the days when newly arrived immigrants swarmed over the city, brotherly love was not one of the attributes of many New Yorkers, who, forgetting their own beginnings, began to consider these strangers as interlopers. The doorman in front of the hotel my father wanted to enter was one of that kind. With a black look at my father, carrying his two suitcases, he refused to allow him to enter the lobby. He indicated the side entrance with a rude gesture.

This dismissal floored my father. I'm afraid he was scarcely prepared for it and what was to follow. He stood his ground. Whereupon the man seized his arm.

"You damned greenhorn," he snarled, "move on." The words were not clear, but the tone was. My father pushed the man away from him.

Luckily, the manager appeared. "What's going on here, Pete?"

"Oh, this greenhorn, here, he won't take the back door."

The manager turned to my father. "What's your business here?" Papa answered in German that he did not understand. The manager repeated the question in Yiddish. When the explanation came that an uncle lived in his hotel, my father was invited to the lobby and asked to wait for confirmation. Yes, there was an uncle, and he was coming down.

That seemed strange to Papa; why wasn't he invited to go up immediately as he had expected. But he sat there, awaiting further developments.

Finally, after what seemed an eternity, the relative appeared. But, unkindest cut of all, he was dressed in street clothes, gloved, hatted, and obviously in no mood to be burdened by an indigent, newly arrived nephew.

For his part, while he waited for his mother's brother, my father's gorge kept rising; and, seeing him in street clothes, obviously prepared to go out, seemed the last straw. Embarassment and humiliation shot through him like a bullet. Then, suddenly, in his pride, even as the uncle came forward, my father picked up his bags and, without a backward glance, walked out into the street.

26

Papa never saw his uncle again.

The day was nearing its end. Street lamps were being lit. On either side, tall buildings towered overhead as he walked quickly along the street toward the El.

It was after seven when my father reached the Hester Street address the policeman had given him. All his courage and willpower must have been required to enter another unknown, possibly painful, situation. He lingered for a moment at the door, and rang the bell.

"Come in, come in," cried a chorus of voices.

My father saw now that he needn't have been concerned. In contrast to the cold reception he received from his uncle, the greeting from these people was warm and friendly.

The family was seated around the kitchen table. A kerosene lamp, hanging from the ceiling, cast a warm glow over the room. At the head of the table sat a man in his middle thirties. He wore a skullcap on the back of his head. His face was creased with a welcoming smile. He arose, extending his hand.

My father introduced himself, "Julius Grunfeld." Then he mentioned the name of his policeman friend. "Sam Grossman," said the man. "Come sit down, have a bit with us, my friend. I can see you just came off the ship." And pointing to a young girl about twelve who had been sitting beside him, he said, "This is Leah, my oldest. And here are my four little Americans, all four born here in this country. My Leah is a little Mameh to the family. My wife, may she rest in peace, died with the youngest here, my little Shmuel—he is two—and this is Yossel, Joey he calls himself. He is in school already. And here is Abie, he will go to school in January, God willing. And here is Jake with the red hair, he is four. All Yeshiva bochers, God willing."

The man spoke Yiddish mixed with some German. "My Leah is the only child not born here. But she will become an American when she marries, God willing. She was four when we came here. Eight years ago it was, in ninety-seven." Sam touched my father on his shoulder. "But again I am talking too much. Come, my friend, sit down. You look tired."

They made room and Papa sat down at the place set for him—his first meal in America. He had not eaten since he left ship that morning. Reminiscing about this day, his first in America, he said how comforting it had been, that warm, uninhibited introduction, so unexpected. They became good friends, Sam and my father. In later years, Sam would occasionally come to visit us on Sundays. "A nice man. A good friend," Mama would say after he had gone home.

The Grossman flat was no better or worse than the average in the city in those early days. There were three rooms. My father occupied the smaller room at the far side of the place, near the entrance door. As he told us, Sam and the four boys slept in the larger room, and Leah opened a bed for herself in the kitchen.

The room allotted to my father was narrow and long. A small potbellied stove stood in the corner, leaving enough space for a chair and an even narrower bed, neatly made and covered. A washstand, holding a basin with a pitcher of water in it, was placed beside the door in front of the window. When his steamer trunk was delivered, the chair had to be removed to allow space for it. One thing that irked my father was the perpetual twilight in the room; only one window, looking out on a small airshaft that allowed very little light. On the other hand, the kitchen was flooded with sun and light. The family spent their days there. Papa was invited to share the kitchen when he liked. He had a home.

3

The Mop-and-Pail Brigade

NOW IT WAS TIME to take inventory. My father's possessions included much variety, but little cash. After paying the first month's rent, including meals which he shared with the family, his cash position was nine dollars lighter. There was a balance of twenty dollars left out of the thirty dollars he had brought with him. Not a great fortune, but hopefully enough to carry him until he could support himself.

His wardrobe was in first-class condition. There were several suits, English made, a greatcoat, some shirts, and a few pairs of gloves. And he had his books. They were lying on the bed: a prayer book, his Bar Mitzvah present from his mother; a few books by Tolstoy; "Dass hohe Lied", the Song of Songs, by Herman Suderman; and I remember his favorite, which he would read to me, Uriel Acosta. There were other authors; I wish I could remember them. Later there would be a problem in finding room for his books. Permission was asked and given to put up some shelves. And this, eventually, became my father's library, right above his bed.

But now, still unpacking, he placed on the bed, along with his books, many pairs of socks, woolen underwear, shirts and heaven knows what else. He smiled as he unpacked, remembering how foolish it had seemed to cart so many clothes to America. But here, now, how fortunate for him the family's foresight had been; he was grateful for the warm clothes. Later, some would find their way to the pawnshop; but that never entered his mind.

In addition, there was a gold watch and chain; a beautifully engraved silver snuffbox, with the year 1872, the year Papa's father had received it from his father; on his finger, a gold ring set with a dark red stone. I still have the silver snuffbox and the ring.

This, then, was my father's fortune: a good wardrobe, his ring, snuffbox, watch and chain and twenty dollars—not much, but sufficient for survival, he thought.

The first two months Papa shared the family meal. By the end of December, with no job in sight, Papa was forced to practice the most rigid economies. With some embarrassed excuse about a new job which would keep him away from the dinner table, he reduced his food expenses. Sam asked no questions, but insisted, "You must have a good, hot plate of oatmeal in your stomach to start the day." Papa could not refuse.

In a nearby delicatessen, fifteen cents bought a good, hearty bowl of lentil or bean soup with tea and honey cake. This was his evening meal. And still no job. That the streets in America were not paved with gold was certain. Week after week went on, his situation was becoming desperate.

Now, his one meal often consisted of that warming dish of oatmeal in the morning, an apple, and a roll, which he consumed in the evening sitting in a nearby park, remaining on his bench until darkness set in. Then, numb with cold, he walked to the delicatessen. He would order tea and sit with the tea till late in the evening. No one paid attention to him. He sat there, warming his hands wrapped around his glass, staring into space.

One by one, his possessions found their way to the pawnshop. Just before Christmas, in went his ring and silver snuffbox. Later his gold watch and chain. The money received for these articles paid his rent, which had been reduced now to one dollar a week. One week he shoveled snow, and next his English greatcoat went to the pawn shop. What can one say? My father was at the end of his rope. The plain fact seemed to be that there were no jobs here for a newcomer without a trade.

Every nerve in his body shrieked to write home for money. His face had become pallid, his eyes were sunken in their sockets. He felt he could no longer go on. But still he could not write. Was it his destiny to perish in the streets of New York? No, a thousand times no! He must hold on. Something was sure to turn up. Something always did. All his life my father was the firm optimist. Something will happen, he would say, and something often did.

Sam Grossman told us how he watched my father brazen it out alone, giving the world no quarter. He knew what was going on, but my father's pride forced Sam to accept the weekly rent, although he would gladly have waited for it. He understood that as long as my father kept up the fiction of an evening job, he could not offer help.

At the end of February, Papa gave up his room.

In one last attempt to conquer this new, stubborn land, Papa decided to hire himself out as a laborer "to work somewhere in the west," he was told. There were tears in Sam's eyes. Of course he would hold my father's belongings until they were sent for. Then Papa joined the group of immigrants who had gathered at the railroad station, waiting to be shipped to this place called The West.

But even that did not work out. In vain my father insisted that he was strong enough and tough enough to do what was expected of him. No, he was too short and too frail. Papa was five-four; not so short, really. Frail, he was.

What to do now? He could not go back to his room. His pockets were nearly empty. There was nothing to do but wander about the city every day until evening, when for ten cents he could get a night's lodging in some flea-bitten downtown hotel. The second week of this,

Papa caught cold. In the morning, shaking with chills and fever, he was rousted out of his bunk. "One night's bed only; come back tonight," he was told. Nothing to do but walk on the street. The city was shivering in the winter's icy blasts. Half mad now with fever, he could barely lift his foot another step. He could go no further. He would lie down in front of that big building there and die.

He was found lying on the steps in front of St. Mark's Hospital, on Twelfth Street, near starvation, barely alive.

My father would always recount this time of merciless suffering in low tones, in hesitating sentences. He could not face those days again, even in his memory. I heard this story several times, And I must say that I was always shocked by the terrible suffering my father endured, too proud, too sensitive, perhaps too stubborn—I can't say which—to ask for help.

How my father came to faint on the steps of the hospital, only God knows. Perhaps Papa's personal God had at long last nudged the fates into action.

That's the way it was all his life. Always in his darkest hour something would happen to rescue him. Papa firmly believed that his gods would come forward to turn the scales in his favor. I'm afraid that my father grew to rely on these miraculous interventions when things went wrong.

"Something will happen," he would say to my mother. "Something always does."

Well, on that day something *did* happen.

My father was revived, put to bed, and questioned. When he recovered and his story came out, he had his first job in America.

He had joined the mop-and-pail brigade in the hospital. The title of porter, a small wage, and a place to sleep came with the job. True, it was a comedown from his former position in life, but curiously enough, it didn't matter any more. This was a new land, with new standards, and new customs. It was time to forget the old life.

This was America!

4

A Mitzvah

THE HESTER STREET TENEMENT where my father lived for the first few months stood in the midst of a heavily populated immigrant area. It was the first stopover for many Jewish families. No one arrived here with more than token funds. They had nothing, these people, but dreams and hopes for the better future this new land could offer. None spoke English, very few spoke any language but Yiddish. It is easy to see why they clustered together and found comfort in the nearness of their countrymen.

The six-story structures in that street were planned for thirty-six tenants, six to a floor. Actually, counting the boarders that were crowded into every available corner "to help pay the rent," no landlord knew how many people lived in his building. But no one counted, as long as the rent was ready on the first of every month.

The Grossman family was unique on their street. They had passed through their painful period of adjustment and had acquired the skill of speaking English, not to mention the four little Americans who were born into the family after they had settled here. Everyone envied Sam. "What a set of boys! May they be a joy to him. A long life to them."

All his life, Sam was very proud of his children. He was never at a loss to brag about their accomplishments. Years later, when Leah, the oldest, became a teacher and married an American, and when all the boys had graduated from City College, people asked "How did they do it? How?"

It was the Grandmother. Certainly Sam was not a rich man. But there *was* the great American dream. And somewhere out of this picture the Grandmother emerged. That indomitable lady, Sam's mother, going into her middle-eighties by that time, fulfilled her own dreams in the achievements of her grandchildren.

There was no stopping her. Twice she went through the Ellis Island ordeal. The first time she had been deported. There was a slight limp, barely noticeable, but there it was, the limp. No use weeping bitter tears. Her sons would find a way—God willing. She would get to America yet.

My father was still living in the Grossman home when that happened.

The problem of getting the mother back into the country was solved by purchasing a cabin-class ticket, and by her wearing a hat instead of the usual kerchief. To this end, Sam and his older brother practiced rigid self-denial to accumulate the necessary money for a second-class ticket for their mother.

Sam explained that cabin-class passengers were examined right there on the ship, the doctors having boarded the liner for this purpose. Cabin-class and first-class passengers were not subjected to the close scrutiny given steerage passengers on Ellis Island. The reasoning was that if they could afford to come in second or first class, obviously they would not become charges of the United States.

By the end of the summer of 1906, my father was still working at the hospital. Sam's mother, now a proud, hat-wearing, second-class passenger, passed through inspection and joined her happy family. The older brother was going to Wisconsin with his family, now that his mother had successfully reached these shores.

Papa was delighted with the lady, who was a spry, gay, youthful sixty-five. She was small, dark-eyed, with a look of natural amiability.

"And it was not a minute too soon," said Sam. "My Leah, she did her best, but the boys were getting out of hand. Too much for her to handle."

It did not take long for the old lady to handle the boys, handle Leah, handle her big, grown-up son.

In time, as the boys grew older, she managed every cent they earned. Joey shined shoes throughout his grammar-school years. His younger brother, Abie, inherited the shoeshine box when Joey graduated. Joey, now in high school, ran errands for the druggist, cleaned the store and made himself useful on evenings and Sundays. For this, he received two dollars. Into the education box it went. Jake sold papers, and young Sammy tagged along, yelling, "Extra! Extra!" Such little businessmen they were. Grandma was the manager. In this way, they could all go to college.

Fanny Grossman was a most outgoing lady. "Perhaps I can help?" she would ask, and though the answer was "No, thank you," she would help anyway. That was how she was. She could smell trouble and unhappiness a mile away. Sooner or later, she would maneuver herself into a position where she could be of help.

She knew the penurious life that had been my father's lot these past months. She knew it continued, although he had the job in the hospital now. And she knew the reason for it.

Having calculated his earnings, my father realized that if he saved every cent it would still be two more years, and perhaps longer, before he could buy cabin-class tickets for his wife and child. And cabin-class tickets were a definite must, he often said. He could not have his family risk possible deportation. Besides, from his personal experience he knew the steerage crossing was hardly fit for animals, much less human beings. He could not allow his family to suffer the stench of un-washed bodies, pressed together in packed bunks, and the pitching motion of the hull, turning stomachs there at the bottom of the ship.

Yes, second-class tickets would have to be provided. To accomplish this, my father practiced the most austere economies. He had extra jobs on his free after-noons to earn money. In the process, he learned English. And already he regarded himself as an American.

In January 1907, a letter for my father arrived at the Grossman's. It was a request to present himself for an interview. If he were still interested in the position, they would see him the following week. He had been highly recommended.

What position? Papa asked. But Sam was as puzzled as my father, who turned the envelope over several times, speculatively. No clue. A joke—that was it—a stupid, foolish joke. That *was* it. But who? He knew very few people. Who of his acquaintances would stoop to this kind of practical joke? Then Sam said, "Go there. It can't hurt. Maybe this man who signs himself Katz and Katz, maybe he's real."

Well, Katz and Katz were real. And then Papa remembered. He had applied for work as a counterman in a delicatessen and restaurant on Second Avenue, about a year ago, it must have been. But why did they wait? He couldn't understand why they waited this long to send for him, or why they remembered him at all.

In the end he went down and saw Mr. Katz. Papa was told the job would be to stand behind the counter and hand out pastrami sandwiches and pickles. But that did not solve the mystery. Who had recommended him so highly?

Sol Katz just smiled mysteriously and asked when he could start. Papa said he would have to give notice at the hospital. He could be ready the day after.

They were sorry at the hospital to see him leave, but understood why he could not give up this opporunity to earn more money. They wished him luck.

Much later, Papa found out how he had gotten his job. Fanny Grossman, Sam's resourceful mother, knew Papa was having a difficult time accumulating enough money to bring his family to this country. She could scarcely stand by idly when so much could be done. The delicatessen Katzes were the nephews of her Rabbi in Vilna, Reb Kreutzinger. The Rebbe had given her a letter saying that she could go to his rich nephews in America if she ever needed anything. She remembered distinctly how Reb Kreutzinger had said, "Go to Katz in America, he is rich. He will help. A mitzvah! You understand?"

She understood. And now was the time to put that letter to the test. Under threat of being stricken dead right on the spot if anyone in the family breathed even one syllable to my father, who could not accept favors, Sam made everyone swear to silence. Sam accompanied his mother to the Katz establishment, and was impressed. "A fine business, may God protect it from harm."

The letter from the Rebbe was produced.

They told the whole story to the Katzes, describing Papa's misfortunes, his fine wife and child waiting in Europe, "God knows in what condition, starving maybe," Fanny's imagination expanded the situation.

41

"You read about these things, you know," she added.

They had lunch. Fanny had sized up the younger Katz, who read and reread the letter from the Rabbi in Vilna. He could hardly keep from crying. His face was twisted in a painful knot. That one has memories, thought Fanny. He will make a job for us.

One of the brothers thought he remembered that a man by that name had been around some months before, asking for work. He had been employed in a hospital. "That's him, my God, that's him!" screamed Fanny. "The poor man, will you give him a job?" She looked around. "It's a busy place, you can find something—" Sol Katz, the older brother, smiled. "Mameleh, don't worry, I will write him a letter. And tell our uncle, the Rebbe, our debt to him is closed. Your friend, he must be something special, that you took so much trouble for him."

And Fanny, with her slight limp, embraced the brothers. "God will be good to you. May you prosper, and your children's children."

A few months later, in May, my father had enough money to bring us to America.

5

The Family Joins Papa

LATE IN THE MORNING of the third of June 1907, the Hamburg-American liner, President Grant, steamed into New York Harbor.

We had crossed the Atlantic, my mother and I, to join my father, who had gone to America "to make his fortune," my mother explained.

Two years before, when we had gone to live with Mama's parents, everyone had expected my father to come back "where he belonged." But as it turned out, he chose to become an American. And Mama often said that she had been very reluctant to follow her husband to America. It seemed unbearable to her to leave her home, her mother and father, her younger sister.

But wives belonged with husbands. Grandfather, grief-stricken though he was, convinced Mama that she should join my father in America.

So Mama wiped her eyes, squared her shoulders, and, spunky lady that she was, set her sights on America and the new life that awaited her across the ocean.

Grandfather, I remember, had slipped an envelope into Mama's hand containing a substantial sum of money. "For you, when you need it most," he said. He had also given us new outfits. I had a sailor hat with long, velvet ribbons trailing down my back. I must admit we travelled well. It was our last luxury for many years to come.

My mother was twenty-five when she left her native country to join her husband in America. I remember a photograph of us taken the day of our departure—my mother, a small, slim, girlish figure, in her stylish grey travel suit, her dark, unafraid eyes looking out into the world from under the brim of her sailor hat encased in a dotted veil. The leggy bit standing beside her in a cloud of embroidered fluffiness was me.

I'm sure we looked very classy when we arrived in Ellis Island and sat waiting for Papa to take us home.

And my father was late.

The minutes passed, one by one. A million catastrophic possibilities assaulted our imaginations.

"Where is Papa?" "Was there an accident?" "Has he forgotten that we were coming?" "Is he coming at all?"

These fantasies took their toll. My mother's eyes filled, and I panicked. "Where is my Papa? Where is my Papa?"

My poor, harrassed mother. Little girls have no conception of the anguish they cause their parents. Fearful of drawing the attention of the immigration officers, my mother availed herself of the one sure course left to her. A sharp, stinging slap, sudden, and unexpected, brought me to my senses. But it was too late. What my mother feared had come to pass. An immigration inspector came upon the scene; perfectly harmless in these days, but not for the immigrant of 1907, who froze in his tracks at the very sight of a uniform—any uniform.

Stories of the most heartbreaking kind had been passed around among the passengers—stories of deportation, and separated families. Deportation could not be ruled out, even for second-class passengers. It was the towering spectre in every immigrant's mind. Complete, convulsive fear of being judged unfit for America created waves of terror in the people who sat waiting for inspection.

Who passes through? Who does not? A wrong word, a tired, dragging foot, an eye reddened by fatigue and tears, hunched shoulders that had been loaded with many a pack, an inadvertent slip that a job was waiting—violating the law designed to protect immigrants from slave labor—any of these exposed the terrified immigrant to a stern examination and possible deportation.

My mother had been warned by Papa above all to appear calm; no crying. Silent weeping was permitted, but no loud outbursts. Hysterical behavior, or any implication of mental disorder, even a slight tremor, could be fatal. That is what Mama had feared at the outset of my tantrum: a suspicion on the part of the officials that my childish hysterics might have been triggered by a mental imbalance.

45

But the inspector looked at my mother for one long moment, passed his eyes over me quickly, pinched my cheek and went his way. Later, we realized that our fine travel outfits had influenced him. If we could afford to travel in style, obviously we would never become public charges.

And then, suddenly, my father was there.

I am ashamed to say that what should have been a dramatically happy reaction somehow developed into a wide-eyed, almost hostile stare. On my part, at least. That could not be my Papa; that was a greying old man whom I did not know at all. Definitely not my Papa who left us with Grandfather to go to America for his fortune. I drew close to my mother, a bewildered little girl.

Two years had blotted out my father's image. I remembered him with different eyes. His hair was black and shiny then. His face was not so thin and pinched. His working clothes were a shock to my mother, I could see.

My mother had drawn her veil up and was blowing her nose. She was weeping. Just at that heartbreaking moment, I was suddenly snatched into two strong arms and kissed. It was my Papa after all. My mother came close and for a moment I thought my father would cry, too.

And so we walked out into America, a small group of three, to start our life in the new land.

Steerage
passengers
sailing from
Hamburg to
New York
in 1906.

Adventurers,
dreamers,
scholars,
beggars—they
came at a time
when the gates
of America
were open
to the world.

48–49

Strength
and courage
were needed
to endure
the steerage
crossing.

When the immigrants reached New York, they had to pass through Ellis Island. My father had heard stories of the ordeal that awaited him there.

52–53

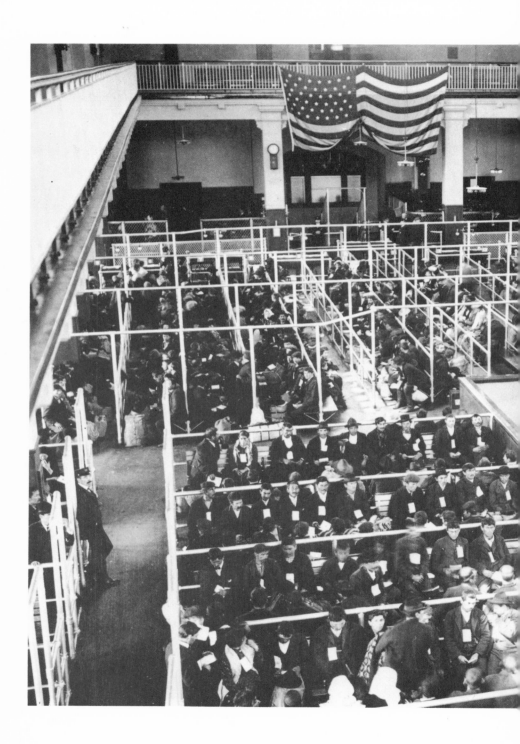

During the peak period of immigration in 1906 and 1907, thousands were examined in Ellis Island every day. Many were detained for possible deportation.

Who passes through,
who does not?...

The spectre of deportation
haunted every steerage immigrant.

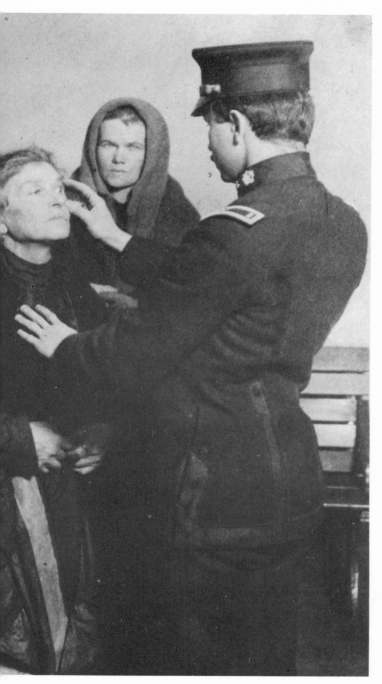

Eyes, ears, chest —
the entire person
was scrutinized
by doctors.
Those who were
turned away
fell into
the depths
of despair.

Those
who passed
found themselves
in Battery Park,
at the end
of a long
journey and the
beginning
of a new life
in America.

6

Four Homes in One Year

W E LIVED in four homes that first year.
We lasted one month in the rooms my father had prepared for us on Ninth Street and Avenue C. That place was unacceptable, even by our diminished standards. The toilets were privies in the cellar, two flights down dimly lit stairs. That was for the Hottentots, my mother declared. "I will look for something better."

My mother was an energetic lady. She began talking to people she met in stores. The grocery store was her most productive source of information; but any information that might possibly lead to another apartment was collected. In the end it was the grocery-store lady who led my mother to our next home.

Incidentally, when we first arrived in New York, and, for quite a few years after, I cannot recall the use of the word "apartment," or even "flat," when people referred to their living quarters. It was always the "place," or the "rooms"—never the "apartment."

But before we left that Ninth-Street place, we had our first experience with the rugged July Fourth celebrations of that time. And a hair-raising experience it was. Someone had told Papa that on that one day, Indians with firearms were brought into the city and given free reign to fill the street with their shooting and savagery. We spent that first July Fourth huddled together in our rooms, trying to understand the fearful din going on outside. I remember my mother hanging a heavy quilt across the window that faced the street, and how frightened we were. Those wild, lusty July Fourths were enough to terrify any European. And Mama was not too certain whether America was for her after all; she was ready to go back home "where civilized people lived."

On the first of August we moved to Seventy-sixth Street and Second Avenue. That apartment wasn't much better, but the toilet was upstairs, a few feet from our door. We shared it with another family who lived across the hall. It was not the best of arrangements, but better than going down those dark cellar steps.

The facilities for taking a bath seemed odd indeed—two washtubs, with a removable center partition. We tried to accept the convertible washtubs as part of the American scene, but bathing became a chore, no fun for anyone—unless he was acrobatically inclined—to climb into the makeshift tub. At first we were amused. If this was the way Americans bathed, who were we to argue.

Later, we learned that many bathtubs in New York City were in bathrooms, and many toilets were private.

By the time we found that out, it was too late; Papa hated moving; and besides, the rent was cheap. When my mother broached the subject, Papa dodged the issue in his usual way; he went back to his reading. The subject was closed.

My mother knew, however, that sooner or later Papa would get sick of the makeshift bathtub. At the end of the summer, she went about finding another flat again, this time with a private bathroom. As usual, the grocery store was her source of information. Yes, there was a very fine place on 92nd Street, boasting its own bathroom. Mama rented the rooms. That evening, realizing she had walked rashly into a situation that would become more difficult with every moment of delay, she went directly to the point. "I have found a place with a private bathroom."

My father laid down his book. "Really? Where?" Suddenly he took in the full meaning of my mother's words.

"You didn't—" My mother shook her head, "I did." "But hear what I have to say before you get angry. There is a bathroom opening onto a hall. But the hall is in the flat. Our personal private hall and bathroom."

The private bathroom was a point that my father could not argue. Then he remembered the moving expenses from Seventy-sixth Street to Ninety-second Street. For this financial problem my mother came up with a happy solution. She had learned of it by accident. It was simply that people who moved withheld the last month's rent to cover the moving expenses. It was done all the time in America. It was the custom. People said that if moving became a necessity, the fault lay with the landlord. Who else? So, let him pay. It was a custom my mother agreed with heartily. America had some fine customs.

My father threw up his hands. What can one do with such a woman?

We moved one month later, on the first of October.

The landlord sighed, and rented the rooms to other tenants. There were no leases those days. At least, not where we lived.

It was a nice enough flat on Ninety-second Street. The kitchen was exceptionally large. My mother liked moving about in large kitchens.

The apartment was located in the rear of the building. All the windows looked down into the courtyard. Most of the winter the yard was covered with snow. But when the snow melted and the warm days of May came, from the yard below rose smells that made it seem as if all the eggs of the world were rotting there. We kept our windows closed whenever possible, but in the heat of summer, when all the windows would be open, what then? Disaster stared us in the face. Mama was ready to move again.

This time the grocery store was no help. My mother was desperate—that awful smell. My father agreed ruefully that other quarters must be found, although he recoiled at the thought of moving again. He had become used to Ninety-second Street. He knew when the elevated train came by, and how long it took him to get to his job; he stopped to chat every evening with the newspaper man who had his stand at the foot of the stairs to the El; and he liked the warm greetings from people in the train who went to work and came home the same time with him every day.

Well, on the first of June, we moved again.

This time, it was my father who found our new home. He had learned of a modern, steam-heated tenement on Eighty-first Street near the East River.

My mother was never one to let grass grow under her feet. The next morning she asked a neighbor, "Is it too far to walk to Eighty-first?" adding, "It is near the river."

No, they were only short blocks, not far at all. My mother took me firmly by the hand and we walked to Eighty-first Street to inspect the rooms in that modern, steam-heated building. Mama was enchanted by what she saw! A white porcelain sink, hot water, a gas stove, and a white bathtub! The vacant rooms were on the third floor. One room faced the street. It was nice to have a room facing the street, Mama said. There were two bedrooms, a kitchen and the "front room." The janitor said the landlord lived in the building.

Mama gave a deposit.

In the evening my father listened to my mother recite the wonders of that marvelous flat. "Imagine, a gas stove for the cooking," Mama was really excited. "When I think of all the ashes I sifted for the coal that

My parents around 1910.

didn't burn, my God! No more ashes to get into everything, a stove that bakes and cooks when you strike a match, I can't believe it."

My father cleared his throat, but no one paid attention. "And there is the bedroom off the hall, a personal private hall, separate; I mean, this room is separate from the rest of the place," she explained.

"That's nice," my father said. "Buy why do we need one room separated from the rest of the family?"

"For the boarder."

"The boarder? What boarder?" My father's voice became shrill, "You didn't rent—you didn't—not with a boarder."

"No, of course not. Where would I get a boarder in such a hurry? I paid a deposit," she added quickly.

My father was stunned. Such fast action was too much for him. He liked to mull things over. But Mama never turned things over in her mind longer than it took her to decide one way or another. Especially when such marvelous things as white sinks, gas stoves and separate rooms for boarders were in jeopardy.

Papa recovered his voice. "How much is the rent?"

My mother squared her shoulders. "Nine dollars."

"Nine dollars." My father's face was getting redder and redder. "My God, do you know what you have done? Nine dollars for rent—I only make eight dollars a week."

"Don't worry—we will manage. It's such a beautiful

place. You will be happy there. Some day you will thank me," she added.

"But that high rent—we only pay seven here."

Two dollars was the difference between eating well and not eating well. A loaf of bread was four cents; a quart of rich, good milk was four cents; a dozen eggs cost ten cents.

Mama revealed her plan.

"We will take a boarder. He will help with the rent."

"No! No boarder!" My father's voice was final. He went back to his paper.

My mother said nothing. When Papa came home on the last day of the month, he found an empty apartment and a note telling him to come to Eighty-first Street. We had packed and moved into that modern tenement with its steam heat, hot water and white procelain sink. Mama had decided to face him with the accomplished fact. And it worked. Everything went along splendidly. My father rang the bell, stepped into his new home as if nothing had happened, washed his hands, and sat down to eat.

It was the fuss and disorder of packing and moving that he hated, and my mother knew that. Later, my father admitted that Mama had been right.

Perhaps I should add that eventually Mama overcame my father's objections to a boarder and rented the hall bed room for two dollars a week. I was transferred to a makeshift bed in the front room.

7

Is This Can for Eating?

THE MODERN TENEMENT on Eighty-first Street in which we now lived was our fourth home, and the last we would have for quite a few years. No one enjoyed that apartment more than my mother. Her housekeeping chores now were considerably lightened. There used to be a weekly painting of the iron sinks to keep them white, and ashes to sift, coal stoves to manipulate, and water to heat for baths.

Mama's particular pride and joy was the gas stove. She presided over that stove like a queen. She would strike a match and hold it proudly to the burner, never ceasing to be delighted when the flame came up. She cooked the most marvelous dishes, and baked her strussel kuchen and those apricot and nut tarts for which she was famous. Not to have to deal with ashes anymore; that was something to be appreciated. ·

The gas for the stove came from a meter that was fastened to the kitchen wall. Papa took care of the gas meter the first day. He slipped a quarter into it and then promptly forgot about it. Well, several weeks went by, and then, late one afternoon, about suppertime, Mama was confronted with an unexpected situation. She put a lighted match to the burner, but no flame came on. "Where is the fire? How can I cook without a fire?" Mama cried, almost in tears with frustration. She had accepted the gas in the stove as a natural part of her new, glorious life in America. Now there was nothing; no fire to get supper started.

"What is the matter with this stove?" she called out to me. "There is no fire!" She struck match after match without results. By this time she was furious. She decided that the new landlord was in no way to be trusted. It looked as though she might have made a mistake in moving into this fine, fancy place. Enraged, she made her complaints loud and clear. "He will get no rent for this month, not one cent," she cried. "And God knows what other disasters we can expect. Go, call the landlord," Mama ordered, turning to me, "he will hear plenty, that goniff. A broken stove he gave us."

When Mr. Resch arrived on the scene, she made her complaints loud and clear. Mr. Resch, our landlord, lived in the building. His rooms were above the saloon, which he also owned.

"What is wrong with the stove?" the startled man asked.

"What is wrong, you ask? Thank you very much. I will tell you what is wrong. It is broken . . . that is what is wrong. There is no fire. How can I cook supper, please tell me, my rich Mr. Landlord, when there is no fire?"

Mr. Resch asked me to bring a quarter. We had no quarter. He dug into his pocket. That poor man, how difficult it must have been to keep his face straight. "Here," he said to Mama, "please put this quarter in that box hanging on the wall, and you will have gas. It is a little trick we have in America to bring gas into the stove."

Mama's amazement knew no bounds. That evening, supper was late. "Will wonders never cease in America," Mama said to my father afterwards. It seemed fantastic to her that a coin slipped into a box hanging on the wall should bring gas into her stove.

Now Mama knew what to do when the gas gave out. After that, it was one great battle between Mama's memory and the needs of her stove. "In the middle of anything I cook," she said, "the gas goes dead." She went on, "How can I remember every minute to have a quarter in the house?"

The following day my father brought home a cut-glass sugar bowl which he had purchased for ten cents in Woolworth's. That sugar bowl was to hold all the quarters that came into my mother's hands. But however desperately she put her mind to remembering the requirements of her stove, it was still nip and tuck between the demands of the gas meter and the contents of that sugar bowl. Suddenly the gas would give out—in the middle of a roast, a stew, a breakfast—it played no favorites. And not a quarter in the sugar bowl. Then the wall of our neighbor's kitchen would resound to my mother's frantic banging. "Mrs. Walsh, please, you have a quarter?" "Oh, sure, come on in." And all this through the wall. Who had a telephone in 1908? Thin walls came in handy those days, if one had a thick skin to go with them.

My father hated the thin walls. He winced at the thought of our family conversations being overheard by our neighbors, and was constantly shushing us to lower our voices. Often there would be an irritated response from my mother. "My God, let me talk—if they hear, how can it harm?" "You don't understand," my father would answer. To which my mother replied, "What is to understand!"

Papa never explained. When my mother seemed insensitive to things that were important to him, he always sighed, "You don't understand."

But Mama went along in her uninhibited way. They were in a new land, where people communicated through dumbwaiter shafts, out of windows, through neighbor's walls. One had to get used to it.

My father did his best. And quietly he came to see his position through my mother's eyes. After all, they were in America. There was no place for their old world customs. And how delighted Mama was with the new ways in America. And I suspect that deep down Papa was no less impressed than my mother with the new ways.

Today, of course, the immigrant is more sophisticated. After all, what newcomer would be floored now by a gas meter in the kitchen—or by a simple tool like a can opener, as my mother was so long ago.

Those sealed cans, standing on the grocer's shelf, intrigued and tantalized her. "That can with the picture of a fish on it, is it for eating?" she asked the grocery man.

"Yes," said the grocer. "I will buy one," said my mother.

She brought the canned salmon home, but nothing in the world got the contents out. She went back, embarrassed but determined. The obliging grocer opened the can for her. The gadget that he manipulated seemed a fearful instrument to her. That is why he opened cans for my mother for the longest time.

After that one could see my mother, walking slowly, very carefully, step by step, holding the opened can far away from her person so as not to spill its potent contents on her dress. Mama was convinced that only an experienced grocery man was sufficiently familiar with the cutting tool to open cans of salmon.

I cannot recall when my mother finally decided to come to grips with her fear. Not much was said, but suddenly a can opener rested in the drawer with the spoons.

One must realize that most of the people coming to

this country at the beginning of the century had never come in contact with canned goods and packaged foods. This was yet another change for the immigrant. But each step, successfully taken, added confidence. The children learned quickly, and the parents followed.

8

My Mother's Secret Job

M Y FATHER, like many other immigrants, never lost some of his European ideas, especially where the role of women in the family was concerned.

There were some heated discussions on this subject after we moved to Eight-first Street, particularly during the period following the depression of 1907 when my father was laid off from his delicatessen job and quarters for the gas meter became scarce. During one of these exchanges, it came out that Mama had been offered a job in a bakery nearby, which she was seriously considering. But my father would have none of it.

"It is for me to provide the money," he said. "Your job is the home."

"I know," Mama said, "and under ordinary circumstances I would agree with you. But we need things for the home, and everything costs so much, and—"

But Papa had already gone back to his paper. The subject was closed. Then, what should have been a stormy response from my mother, unexpectedly became a tight-lipped silence.

That was strange—no counter argument? This was not like her. To keep quiet when she felt herself to be in the right was not her style. Why?

The following day an even stranger thing happened. I found the door locked when I returned from school. For the first time in my life, my mother was not there when I came home. Mama not home? At this time of day? This was really unusual. But there was Mama, running breathlessly up the stairs, carrying a bag of groceries.

"My God!" she cried. "Already you are home?" There was not time for my glass of milk and bread-and-butter sandwich that afternoon. Instead, I was told to be a good girl and make the beds so Mama could get supper ready in time. I made them and went back to set the table. Why had Mama been so late? It was not like her to leave the house in disorder. She had always been a meticulous housekeeper. Meanwhile Mama swept the kitchen floor, pushing the dust under the dish closet. This really shocked me. Never did my mother sweep anything under anything!

Those frantic scrambles to get things done later in the afternoon went on, day after day, and all Mama ever said was, "My God, how short the day is. Where does the time go?"

For this little girl it was very frightening. The orderly world I had been accustomed to had suddenly changed. And though I asked no questions, I could not help wondering.

Suddenly I understood. My mother had a secret job.

And I was warned not to tell Papa.

Every morning, after we left the house, I to school and Papa to his job, my mother would go to the small bakery on Avenue A, now York Avenue. The way she looked at it, she had exchanged her culinary talents for money. It was either that or trips to the pawnshop. She chose the job. Papa's salary had to be supplemented somehow.

This went on for several months, and I said nothing. Then in some way—I cannot recall how—Mama's secret bakery job came to my father's attention.

Papa was angry, but his anger gave way to hurt resentment. It was not the job itself, he said, although that was bad enough. Outside work was completely out of bounds for a lady, and he was surprised that Mama had so soon forgotten who she was.

"And you knew about Mama's job?" I nodded, and Papa's face turned to stone.

"Why? How could you do this? When you knew my feelings about this?" Mama cut in, "Don't blame the child. But money has had to come from somewhere. A boarder you objected to. What else was left but to pawn some more silver? You need money for the lodge, the child needs shoes . . ."

"But you have money . . ." Papa could get no further.

"That is for a rainy day. I will not touch it."

This was the thousand kroner that Grandfather had slipped into Mama's hand before we left Yarac for Hamburg. That money became her personal "nest egg" for a "rainy day"—though in all the years it never rained hard enough for my mother. Never!

"Do as you wish," Papa said in a hurt tone, "but understand that when you hire yourself out, I am shamed."

My mother gave up the bakery job. She did not want to shame her husband.

It was a difficult decision for Mama. Times were hard in the aftermath of the depression of '07. Many people were laid off, as was my father eventually. Banks were closing, savings were wiped out. And there were bleak days in our house. I remember huge pots of bean soup and garlic bread which my mother served grandly in a soup tureen. Every day for some time she brought that soup tureen to the table, changing bean occasionally for lentil or split pea. But what I remember most vividly from this period was the bean soup and garlic bread.

Papa worked at many jobs that year, but never anything permanent. He was a waiter for a short time in a North Beach resort hotel, coming home only on his afternoon off. He worked at whatever was available.

Toward the end of the year our luck changed. Papa began working in the shipping department of a German-American import and export house, packing fine china and glassware.

How that job came his way, I have no idea. But there were no jobless days after that for many years.

9

The German School

IN SEPTEMBER of the year we moved to Eighty-first
Street, I was enrolled in P.S. 96, a complete dodo as
far as the English language was concerned. I remember
sitting in that classroom, alone and miserable, knowing
only a few words of English, without a single friend. I
had no choice but to learn the new language, quickly
and without fuss. Not much help was offered. Few
teachers were linguists, and the feelings of the
greenhorns in the class were not spared. This method
led to miracles of accomplishment.

If the teacher occasionally had a difficult child to deal
with, a note to the parents would result in fast and permanent reform. Misbehavior in school was considered a
disgrace upon the family. Parents had nothing but the
highest respect for teachers, who were looked upon with
awe and admiration. If our parents were greeted by a
teacher walking down the street, they felt honored. I
remember that teachers carried themselves with great
dignity. Next to doctors, they occupied the highest place
in our immigrant world.

The author as a schoolgirl in P.S. 96.

In the beginning, the first year, my father insisted that at home I speak German. For some time I was obliged to lead a double life. In school, I had to speak English; with my parents I could only speak German. With my friends, I spoke whatever language came into my head.

At home there was the tug between the old and the new. In the front room, where I did my homework on the round oak table, I was immersed completely and utterly in the English language. After homework was finished, German took over. My father did not want to cut himself off completely from his past, and, he said, "Anyway, it is part of education to speak at least two languages."

It was now almost inevitable that Papa should join the Turnverein, on Eighty-second Street, the lodge for German-Americans. Soon he discovered to his delight that a private German class was in progress in the Turnverein. The class was held in the Mozart Hall on Eighty-sixth Street, between Second and Third Avenues, which is still standing.

Papa promptly enrolled me. I was nine years old. The prospect of going to a second school three times a week from four to six seemed most unpleasant. I appealed to my mother, but Papa was adamant. My fate was sealed.

Every other afternoon I walked to Eighty-sixth Street and the German class, which I hated. Now, of course, I have to admit that it was the best thing my father could have done. In those immigrant days the education of most girls ended in grammar school. The career of a girl

The Mozart Hall on 86th Street in Yorkville.

was marriage; no other career was acceptable. This was the thinking of the day. But since I was a good student, and my father never conformed entirely to the conventional wisdom, the higher education offered by the German school seemed an acceptable compromise for me. Mr. Winter, the teacher and principal, drilled into me more Latin, composition, literature, history and mathematics that I could have acquired in any other way, considering that my formal education ended in the eighth grade.

Report cards were issued regularly. I still have those unusual documents in my possession—unusual for their size, about ten inches square, and unusual for their careful evaluation of our scholastic abilities. The ratings were one to five. One was excellent. Mine were all One's, except for attendance.

I was a good scholar in most subjects, but music appreciation escaped me then, and escapes me now. I like a good tune, but that is where the appreciation ends. I must have been a painful thorn in Mr. Winter's side, because, in a little note he sent to my parents he wrote, "Your child would do better in the kitchen, cleaning pots."

Mr. Winter was a tall, loosely hung, bony man, with thick eyeglasses and a great deal of explosive impatience, especially during music periods. My father soon learned that he gave private music lessons at his home for twenty-five cents a week. As a result, once a week, on a Saturday, I walked to Mr. Winter's home on

Eighty-third Street near Second Avenue, for mandolin lessons, of all things. My father happened to have a friend who had sold him a mandolin, cheap. Musical instruments were musical instruments; to his way of thinking, one was as good as another. So I took mandolin lessons. It was a most unrealistic dream of my father's, as he eventually discovered.

For several years I romped with the other children. Suddenly the fun became stale. I discovered books.

The library on Seventy-eighth Street and Avenue A was near enough for me to bounce in and out with an armful of books, between schools. To my surprise, one by one, my friends became strangers. I could not understand why. There seemed no explanation for the resentment my reading caused. My feelings were in a turmoil. Suddenly my friendly world had changed. I was regarded as a kind of freak. The music lessons made it worse, when, on Saturdays, I walked through the street carrying the mandolin. But even as I held my head high, inside I thought I would die. It was a horrible time for me. Then, unexpectedly, my father, after a private talk with Mr. Winter, gave up the idea of making a musician out of me.

German classes continued, however. Still, life was easier now that the mandolin was laid away. My books no longer aroused so much antagonism. The street and I became accustomed to one another again.

And I acquired a friend. I met Esther Liebhoff at the end of April, when the trees in Central Park were in

Every year
on the
first of May
we danced
around
the Maypole
in Central Park.

their full spring glory. The Liebhoffs had a drugstore on the corner of Eighty-first Street and Avenue A. Esther and I became partners in the traditional Maypole dances that were organized by our teachers in Central Park to celebrate May Day. Round and round the colorful Maypole we hopped and skipped; two little girls as different as day and night.

In September, Esther joined me in German school. Every other afternoon, we skipped happily to our German classes. German school took on a different dimension. I was no longer alone. Together, we faced the world with a smile, we found everything exciting and funny.

I went to German School for four years, until my father, with his European ideas, decided I'd had enough education to last me a lifetime. He added that there was a job waiting for me in his firm, with the salary of four dollars a week to start.

There was no arguing. Papa had made up his mind. I went to work in the showroom of L. Barth and Sons, the import-export firm where Papa was employed. My job was to dust the samples in the showroom; shelf after shelf of expensive crystal and china. It was extremely nerve-wracking. I lived in constant fear of dropping one of those fragile things.

After three weeks I left.

Papa was angry, but not as furious as I had expected. Resuming my studies was out of the question to him, but I did not have to return to the showroom. Instead, I started to work in a small dry goods store in the neighborhood. I kept the books and the inventories, and helped with the selling. The owner was very kind; he taught me the fundamentals of business, and after a while he came to depend upon me. I enjoyed it.

A college education always seemed to me to be the ultimate in achievement. Since I never went to college, I am in no position to speak from personal experience; still, I always felt that I was deprived of something special in life. I've never lost a feeling of awe for those venerable halls of learning; a corner of my life left unfulfilled.

But no regrets; I lived in a different era.

After I started work, Esther and I saw each other less often. Sometimes she came into the store and we pretended that things were the same, that nothing had changed. But our old friendship had been dealt a fatal blow. We drifted apart.

I remember that friendship with great affection. How we laughed, my friend Esther and I. Fortunately, I have not outgrown this bent toward the absurd. I like to think that in later years, when hard times and then tragedy made life seem unbearable, I was strengthened by it in some small way. How foolishly we squander our laughter in the first flush of youth. Some of it should be stored for later use, when responsibilities and disappointments and grief weigh us down.

10

The Yorkville Melting Pot

THOSE OF US who lived in the east Eighties during those early years of this century may remember the Christmas pushcarts that lined First Avenue in November, heralding the holiday season. For the immigrant, who had very little to spend, the pushcarts held the most marvelous, exciting promise of things to buy. An image comes to me of my mother puttering about among the wares, seeking the inevitable bargain, a shirt for my father, a blouse for herself, perhaps a dress for me; on the pushcart in front of Rosenberg's dry goods and department store.

The pushcart must seem utterly without meaning in these days of lavish department store displays. But for us a need was filled at Christmas time by the gaily decorated wares that were spread out by the street merchants. There were splashes of green pine trimmed with red holly, giving the appearance of a wooded section in the midst of the city grey. And that was something for us children, who rarely saw the green of a tree, and almost never the golds, the browns, and the oranges of autumn leaves.

And that delicious fragrance of freshly roasted chestnuts. One cent bought a bag of eight hot chestnuts, split in the middle. Nothing in all the world ever tasted so good.

Most fruits and nuts were a luxury. Oranges miraculously appeared once a year, in Christmas stockings. And bananas —I never saw a banana until years later, when Mama could afford to be extravagant now and then.

Here I was on the street with my Christmas money—five cents, to spend as I liked. Five cents, tightly clutched in mittened fists, opened a wide world of goodies. But what to buy? One cent bought eight cherry or lemon drops, two cakes, a bag of chestnuts, or a bag of jelly beans. It was fun.

For a short while I was allowed to pursue my own course while Mama chatted with a neighbor. I flitted about between pushcarts in the first flush of financial independence. I remember the general hustle and bustle, the happy faces of the mothers, my own joy in the decision of my last purchase. At the end of the afternoon, the five cents were spent. In my pocket I had a bag of lemon drops for my father, some jelly beans for Mama; small sacrificial expenditures made in the holiday spirit.

Suddenly, Mama was at my side. It was time to go home. The afternoon had slipped away. There was no more money to spend.

When I hear of those huge allowances that have become weekly parental obligations, I think back to the five cents my mother placed into my hand with the admonishment, "Hold it tight in your hand, Liebchen, Papa works hard. Be careful what you buy."

Weekly allowances for children were unheard of in our neighborhood. The family shared what there was. In many homes, small Christmas gifts were the only money the children ever received. It was all that families could afford. And it is amazing how little the children expected. They didn't miss anything, they didn't ask for anything. There were no questions.

I know that in my childhood home I would never have questioned either my father's judgment, or my mother's. Acceptance of parental authority was essential in those early days. These immigrant parents were completely absorbed in the struggle for survival; they had no energy left for struggling with their children as well. The children understood the harsh conditions, and it never occurred to them to question the way their parents lived. Life was too difficult.

Gentile, Jew and nonbeliever—all were bound by the same pain of Heimweh, the homesickness. All came from somewhere else, all had been strangers once, all had memories of loved ones left behind and waiting. It was not easy to endure the homesickness. But endured it had to be. Life had to be lived.

There was something very real and deep in our early lives in that Yorkville neighborhood—a genuine feeling of acceptance, a real value placed on friendship. My parents enjoyed warm friendships with their neighbors, friendships that began during their first years in America and lasted until they died. It was an era when leisure time was for visiting with friends and neighbors, when good talk was valued over a congenial cup of coffee.

People shared their experiences—their joys and sorrows. Neighbors visited back and forth on a Sunday afternoon; it was the thing to do. Guests were always welcome, and coffee pots steamed on every stove. In our house, on special occasions, a precious bottle of Schlivowitz was brought out, and toasts were drunk to happy futures.

Pleasures were simple in those days. Sunday afternoons, pinochle games were started on the oilcloth-covered table in the kitchen. They were friendly games. Scores were kept on a pad, but no money was passed. Invitations were not issued; the visits were never preplanned. People came to the door, were welcomed, and before anyone was aware, the neighbors sat at our table with Papa, playing cards.

The ladies sat in the front room with a bit of gossip of the day, viewing the America they lived in through their European eyes, comparing, sometimes crying a little when they talked about those left behind.

As I look back to those early days, one thing stands out clearly. For the immigrant who came to these United States at that time, to be an American was the essence of his need, and, unfortunately, also his dilemma. On the one hand there was the pull of the old country, still so fresh in memory; on the other hand, the reality of the new life to be lived—the daily struggle, the striving for betterment, the running to night school to absorb a smattering of the new language, the occasional layoff when savings quickly disappeared; and, late at night, the final closing of doors in each home, when weary mothers and fathers lay down to their hard-earned rest.

It was the time of great ideas and aspirations, of great plans and dreams, of great opportunities and fulfillments.

It was the mystery and magic of America.

Automobiles were
a rarity in
New York
in the early years
of the century.
Transportation was
by shank's mare,
the horsecar...

. . . or the El.

The horsecar
was a smaller
version
of a trolley,
drawn by
two sturdy
mares.

But it did not take
too long before the
small, friendly
horsecars were
replaced by electric
trolleys . . .

which
gave way
in turn
to the
air-polluting
buses.

Another scene
to remember
was the passage
of the horse-drawn
fire engines and
the thunderous
hoofbeats of the
huge horses as
they raced
through the
streets.

But even during
that pre-World-
War-I period,
the old ways
of life in New York
were changing.
As the horses
disappeared,
some of the
warmth
in our lives
disappeared
with them.

11

Paprika Weiss

To the friendless immigrant, New York often was a nightmarish experience—a real hell. It isn't to be wondered, then, that he instinctively sought a group of his own people to settle with. He became attached to his locality, only leaving it when necessary, and then mainly for his job. Once his work was finished, he hurried back to familiar ground.

Such accumulations of kindred souls dotted the city. Our neighborhood in Yorkville was one of them. It was a cluster of German, Jewish, Irish, Czech and Italian immigrants. Most of us remained in that neighborhood year after year. Few families moved away. People were firmly entrenched in their homes, with the same need for belonging as they had had in the old country, where generations often spent their lives in their villages without ever going away.

Our "village" consisted of a few blocks on the East Side in the Eighties. On the northeast corner of Eighty-first Street and Avenue A (now York Avenue), opposite our house, stood my school, P.S. 96. Crossing Avenue

A, diagonally opposite the school stood Liebhoff's drug-store. Going south along Avenue A were the barber shop with its twirling pole, a small family bakery, a shoe repair shop, and a second-hand furniture store.

Many small stores took care of our needs. Super-markets did not exist. Everyone had a close personal relationship with the neighborhood grocer, who often became a banker when hard times came. Records of purchases were carried in small, red-covered notebooks. People shook hands, promised to pay when they could, and they did.

These family groceries were small, unassuming shops, looked after by hard-working owners who were present from dawn until dark, starting their day with the milkman. Our grocer was Mr. Schlutzki, on Eighty-first Street down the block from our house. Early in the morning, you could hear the clatter of the milk wagon going down the street to deliver two forty-quart cans of milk which were set down on the sidewalk in front of Mr. Schlutzki's store. You knew then that it was five o'clock and that Mr. Schlutzki would be hurrying along soon with impatient steps to open his store. A small, ro-tund man, he would carry the milk cans inside, come out a few minutes later, broom in hand, look at the sky to estimate the chances of rain, and begin sweeping the sidewalk in front of the store. That meant he was open for business.

Everything in these grocery stores was sold in bulk; no pre-packaged, pre-weighed merchandise. There were open sacks of flour, beans, rice, and coffee leaning against the wall toward the rear of the store. Butter came in large, wooden tubs, from which the grocer skillfully cut the desired amount, rarely missing by even an ounce. Five cents for a quarter-pound. Eggs were ten cents a dozen. Cheeses were cut to order; there were Swiss and Limburger. Cottage cheese—pot cheese then—came in a large tub.

Milk was four cents a quart, ladled directly out of the big cans. It was untouched by pasteurization and homogenization. Mr. Schlutzki would stir the milk with an enormous scoop to make sure the cream was well mixed. Then he filled the pitcher we brought with us. After we got home, the thick, rich cream would rise to the top.

Unsanitary—unacceptable today—I know. But since we did not know better, we muddled through good, rich milk—germs and all.

In addition to the grocer, invariably somewhere near-by were the butcher, kosher butcher, greens store never far behind, and nestled in between, the candy store, which, for some reason, always seemed to be run by an elderly person—either a man alone or a woman alone. These poor little establishments dispensed penny candies, pencil boxes, penny ice cream sandwiches, cigarettes and little toys. Ice cream cones came later.

A landmark I shall aways remember was the ice and coal cellar, where Frank Trotta, the owner, expected customers to write their orders on a pad to which a pencil was attached with a long string. Now, what could have been more convenient?

No one bought ice during the winter months. At the end of September, boxes appeared outside of windows, fastened in some miraculous way to the window ledge. In these boxes perishables were kept fresh. Why buy ice, when Jack Frost supplied it free. It was not until the early twenties that window boxes disappeared from the scene. In the winter the iceman sold coal and neighborhood furniture, which he traded.

On First Avenue and Eighty-third Street stood Rosenberg's dry goods and department store. Rosenberg's sold everything at bargain prices. Anything on this earth could be found in that store, my mother often remarked. "A real 'schlaghaus,' " she would say.

Mama never passed without stopping to chat with Mr. Rosenberg, an affable round-faced man with handlebar moustaches, not at all the energetic, sharp type one would expect in an establishment of this kind. Mama rarely left the store empty-handed. Her eyes would spot something that seemed a little damaged; a pot slightly dented, or a pair of slippers faded from the sunlight. Always the practical one, she never let a bargain slip through her hands. Nothing was brought into the house unless it was damaged in some way. A spot on a dress—how much? No, that was out of the question, Mama argued. Mr. Rosenberg insisted. He could not reduce it, not one cent. This was to be my birthday gift. Washed and ironed, with a bow covering the bad spot, it would become a wonderful dress. Mr. Rosenberg cut the cost in half.

Next door to our building at 534 East Eighty-first Street was Fleischmann's Vienna Bakery. Here I stood on many a day when I did not go to German school, waiting for the side door to open. Fleischmann's sold us day-old bread for four cents a loaf. Rolls were a penny each. Sweet, buttery-tasting buns, seven for a nickel. My how good everything tasted! Another of those day-old purchases was the huge, round pinwheel kind of bun that my mother called "Schnecken," which means "snails," because that is what they looked like. They were absolutely delicious. These days I see those cakes, still called "snails," in the store, but my old zest for them is gone. That marvelous, buttery flavor seems to have disappeared.

Then there was Paprika Weiss, the Hungarian grocery, still in business on Eighty-first Street and Second Avenue. Paprika Weiss carried various spices and herbs that found their way into Mama's soups, stews, and, of course, the apricot cakes and strudels. Their specialty was a very strong, very red paprika, which we could not get at the grocer's in our street—and that delicious sweet of my childhood, called corn sugar, which both my father and I loved.

For some reason, that store held a special fascination for me. As I think back, one of the incentives was "something good to eat" that came from the man who ran the store, "for you, for being a good girl for your

114

mama," I was told. Whereupon I would leave the store with my purchases, munching my gift of a piece of corn sugar, or a handful of raisins, or a wonderfully juicy pickle fished out of a barrel standing near the door.

Mama didn't take kindly to the pickle juices that ran down my middy blouse. But the pleasure of eating that pickle seemed worth the punishment. The first luscious bite made it seem the most exotic of all foods.

Well, time did not stand still. The years passed. Paprika Weiss became a shadowy memory.

Only now, once again, more than a half-century later, that small child, who was rewarded with a juicy pickle for "being a good girl," stands, a grey-haired lady, in the Paprika Weiss store and buys a very strong, very red paprika, and, in a wave of nostalgic remembrance, glances toward the door. But there stands no pickle barrel.

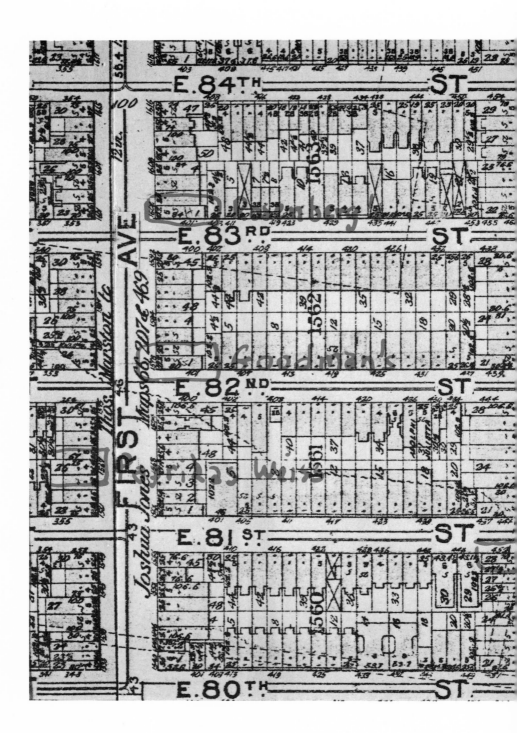

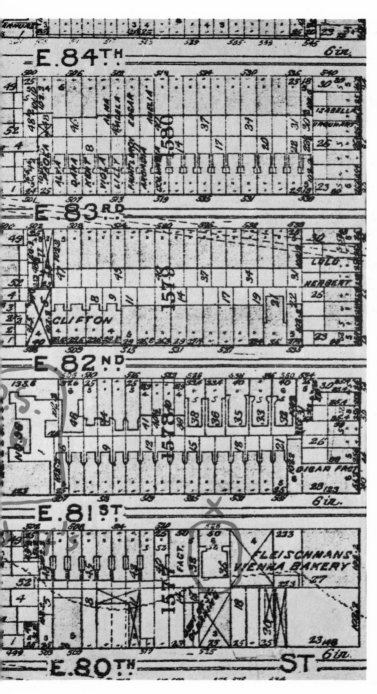

"X" marks the house where we lived for many years. We never wandered far from our neighborhood. P.S. 96 was across the street. Goodman's drugstore was a few blocks away. Fleischmann's Vienna Bakery, next door, was managed by Raoul Fleischmann, who later became the first publisher of the *New Yorker*.

116–117

It seems to me
there was always
a policeman in view,
either standing
on the corner
or walking
up and down
the street.
He knew everyone.
If a loud
family quarrel
erupted, someone
would fetch him
to straighten
things out.
No one was ever
arrested.

The corner
policeman
was the
friend of the
neighborhood.

12

House Calls a Dollar, Office Visits Fifty Cents

N<small>O OLD-TIMER</small> who lived in the East Eighties could ever forget Goodman's Drug Store.

Goodman's was on First Avenue and Eighty-second Street. Never was there such a drug store anywhere in the world. Goodman's had everything from herbal teas to mustard plaster to cures for "Hexenschuss," the terrible "witch's bullet," German for arthritis. A thousand and one calamities were taken care of. First-aid salves healed swollen fingers, wounds were cleaned, scraped knees were doused with peroxide, with comforting words accompanying the awful sting. Somehow we children were never quite convinced that the pain was all that necessary. Mr. Goodman would cure our doubts with the offer of a lollipop.

Another of Goodman's remedies was castor oil, known as Fletcher's Castoria. Mothers swore by its therapeutic powers. Cod-liver oil was not far behind. Our noses were held, and down went the vile stuff. Our parents operated on the premise that if it tasted bad it was good for you.

For more serious illnesses, such as a sore throat that did not respond to salt-water gargling, we were dispatched to the clinic in the German Hospital on Seventy-sixth Street and Lexington Avenue. There we were taken care of for ten cents. Later the German Hospital became the Lenox Hill Hospital.

I was in that predicament with an infected throat when I was about eleven years old. My mother decided that the clinic was necessary. Together we sat waiting in the reception room, where several white-robed figures appeared carrying some sinister looking objects in their hands. One of the doctors approached us. That was enough for me. My heart stopped beating, and suddenly I discovered that my throat was healed. Another instant passed, and I ran. Out the door I flew, with Mama close behind. I reached Third Avenue, Second, First, Avenue A. I never stopped running until I reached our building and hid under the stairs. When my exhausted mother reached the house, loudly promising dire punishment, self-preservation kept me concealed in my hiding place. Mama suspected, of course, where I had hidden; she had discovered me under the stairs before. Never, never had I seen her so angry. Finally, when I concluded that Mama's ire had cooled somewhat, I came out, expecting the world to fall down upon my head. But, as I remember it, punishment was postponed. Mama must have been too exhausted. When my father came home I was put to bed, humbled, salt-water-gargled.

My tonsilitis healed. I did not go back to the German

Hospital and, happily, I still have my tonsils.

People didn't run to the doctor very often those days. If you were bedridden and too sick to go to the clinic, then someone went to fetch him. Nobody can fetch a doctor today; you have to go to his office. If you can't walk, he sends an ambulance. In those early years, there was never any trouble in getting a doctor to the home when illness struck. It went this way.

Someone would run to the doctor, leave his message, and be told "the doctor will be there as soon as he can." Our doctors had neither nurses nor receptionists; nothing as grand as that. But there were wives, mothers, brothers and sisters to take messages.

Nor did our homes have telephones, nor cars in garages. Shank's mare was our transportation. But it worked out fine; no telephone, no automobiles, but invariably there was somewhere a doctor within running distance.

House calls were one dollar. Office visits, fifty cents.

I myself became familiar with this routine when illness suddenly struck my father.

Papa had an iron constitution. I never knew him to be sick. True, there was a sniffle here and a pain there, but as far as he was concerned, it was never anything to get excited about. And he would go to work. But came a March day when Papa arrived home with a noticeable limp.

"Why are you walking this way?" screamed my mother, who was not known to be a lady of great restraint. "It is your knee? It could be you have maybe rheumatism?"

"What rheumatism?" my father scoffed. "Rheumatism is for old men. I am not yet fifty. What do I want with rheumatism? It is only the winter weather that gets into your bones, what else?"

My poor mother. All through supper her face was clouded with worry. Afterwards, my father went to his rocking chair as he usually did in the evening to read the paper. He did his best to maneuver that short distance from the kitchen to the front room without limping, but his face showed the strain. It did not escape my mother's eyes.

"We have a problem," she said to me while we did the dishes. "Papa will never admit it, but I think he has rheumatism. Maybe tomorrow he will have to stay in bed, and then we will get the doctor."

"But Papa will never stay home."

"I know," Mama sighed. "Stubborn like an ox he is, but that bad knee must be cared for. Tomorrow morning we will see."

Well, in the morning my father went to work. My mother could do nothing with him. "I must get to my job," he said. "I'm really all right. They expect me. There is a shipment of fine glass—they depend on me to pack it—you understand?"

My mother nodded—

"I understand. Only, I mean, is there no one else, when all of a sudden you have a little rheumatism—"

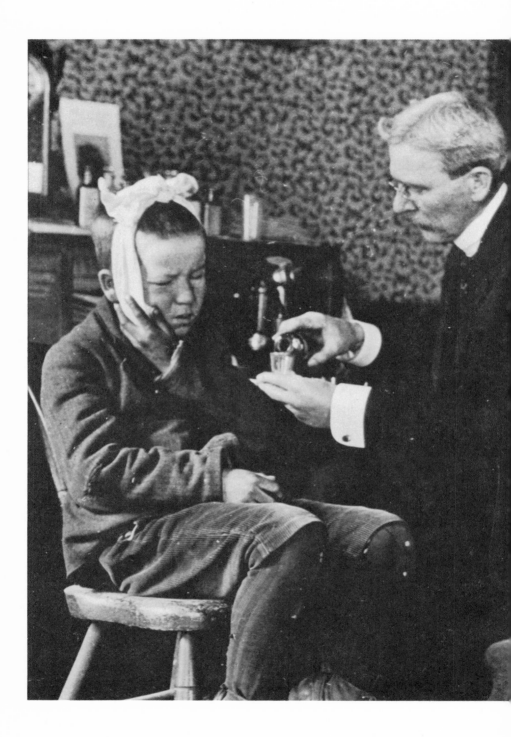

*In those years,
there was never
any trouble in
getting a doctor
to the house.*

"Again with the rheumatism!" Papa shouted. "All right," he admitted, calmer, "the knee is a little swollen. But a man ought to be able to take a little swollen knee, it seems to me. You know, it is only the winter weather that gets into your bones—what else?"

Well, that day, the day he went to work with the bad knee, my father's world of robust health, as he had known it all these years, collapsed into the unfamiliar world of invalidism. When he came home in the evening, he could barely manage the stairs to the third floor, where we lived. His face was ashen and drawn with the exertion of the climb. At the sight of him, standing in the doorway like a ghost, my mother threw up her arms.

"My God! What have you done to yourself?"

She got Papa to bed, asking me to heat the flatiron.

"And bring a hot, wet towel. I want to iron that inflamed knee."

And deep into the night, she passed the heated iron gently over the wet towel that covered that knee. She said it was an old remedy that the folks back home used for rheumatic pains. That—and "a good, strong, hot grog—to sweat it out," she added. My mother had great faith in the "sweating out" process.

Sometime during the evening she brought a large cup of that hot brandy and sugar and water mixture to my father's bedside. He said that his knee felt better and that the grog was just right. Soon he was asleep.

In the morning Papa said he felt much better and

wanted to get up. He got out of bed, walked a few steps; his knee caved in, and he fell to the floor. There was a scene. We reached out to help him. Angrily he pushed us aside, shouting, "Leave me alone! I will not have it, do you hear!"

Mama motioned to me and we left the room. When we came back later, he was lying in bed, pretending to sleep. My poor, embarrassed father, who could not endure his illness, had crawled back into bed. And all my mother could say was,

"My God! My God! How will this end?"

Later we found that his right arm had become stiff. He could barely move it. I was told to run to Goodman's "and bring back something to rub in."

I brought back a black, strong-smelling salve—from Goodman's catalog—which was promptly used.

That was crazy I thought. Why not get a doctor? My mother must have read my mind, because suddenly I heard her declare that she was going for the doctor.

"No, no doctor—no doctor!" Papa cried. "It is only the New York weather that gets into your bones. I'm not really sick," he insisted. "That stink you rubbed in helped. See?" He moved his arm, "Look, already my shoulder is better. What do I want with a doctor?"

He turned his head, and Mama beckoned to me to leave the room with her.

Within the hour, my mother put on her hat and coat and told me to "take care of Papa. I am going for the doctor. And I will bring him back. If he is not there, I will wait for him."

Surprisingly, my father said nothing. He looked at Mama and I think I saw relief passing over his face. He had finally acknowledged that his illness was something he could not deal with.

My mother did not come back for a long time. The doctor was away on house calls when she got there, and as she had promised, she sat in his office and waited for him to return. Two hours later she showed up.

All this while my father was in a vile mood. He fretted and fumed between moans and groans. "Two hours it takes to walk to Seventy-ninth Street?"

I reminded him that Mama was probably sitting in the doctor's parlor waiting for him.

"But two hours?" Papa kept saying. "Two HOURS!"

At last we heard a key unlocking the front door.

"That must be Mama," I said, just to break the tension.

"Two hours you are gone!" my father said angrily the instant he laid eyes on Mama. "Where were you, I would like to know." Papa was really in a fury.

He did not seem to have noticed the doctor, who was standing behind my mother in the doorway.

"So, this is your husband who was dying," the doctor said to my mother, who had implied that the illness was mortal.

"Well, no matter, I am here now. I can see that you meant well—but it was a shameful deception that you resorted to—"

"I know—I'm sorry," Mama interrupted. "But what else could I do? Would you have come right away if I told you only that my husband was sick?"

"Probably not. I would have had my dinner first," said the doctor, doing his best to look severe.

I don't believe that mother was too disturbed by her small exaggeration. She did what, according to her own conscience, she had to do. Her husband needed help. Scruples did not enter into it.

The doctor turned to my father. "Well, let me have a look at you. I'm Rochmeier," he introduced himself.

My mother was instructed to boil a spoon in water for five minutes. That she did not like.

"I always wash my spoons in hot water," she said. "The water in this house is very hot, Herr Doctor."

Dr. Rochmeier smiled . . . "I don't doubt it, madam. But for your husband's throat I need a boiled spoon."

"Oh," Mama said.

She brought the doctor a boiled spoon wrapped in a clean napkin. Then my mother and I were banished to the kitchen. Dr. Rochmeier shut the door in our faces.

Dr. Rochmeier took his time examining my father. The waiting was difficult. Mama sat at the table in the kitchen, steadily tapping the table with her hand. Occasionally a loud sigh escaped her. There was no sound but the ticking of the clock on the shelf, and the steady, nervous tapping.

At last we heard the doctor's footsteps. My mother rose from her chair.

"Sit down, please," he ordered, seating himself at the table opposite my mother. "I want you to stop worrying and listen."

"My husband," Mama interrupted. "Is he very sick? I mean, doctor, will he get cured?"

"Well, I'll tell you," Dr. Rochmeier answered slowly, "your husband has an acute attack of rheumatism. He will get well. But he must stay in bed at least one, and maybe two weeks. And two more weeks in the house, before he goes back to work. And a light diet, please. No meat soups, no chicken soup."

"No chicken soup?" Mama repeated incredulously.

"No meat soups of any kind. For your husband, chicken soup is poison."

"How can that be? Back home we always—"

The doctor smiled, and my mother did not finish what she started to say. She looked at Dr. Rochmeier, her expression showed clearly that she considered her husband's future not too bright if he were in the hands of a doctor who banished chicken soup.

Dr. Rochmeier fished a box of pills out of his bag.

"One pill three times a day," he instructed. "Here in America, we take pills. And keep applying that liniment I smell. But apply gently, you understand—very gently."

Mama nodded her head.

"And wrap some woolen thing around that knee. But it must be wool, you understand, only wool."

Mama nodded her head again.

132

"Nothing like wool to generate heat and get the circulation going."

A fine•smile appeared on the doctor's face. "It is an old remedy I learned from my grandmother. She, too, suffered from rheumatism." His face became stern again. "Now remember, one pill, three times a day. And an old woolen piece around that knee, after you apply the liniment—and no chicken soup."

Mama nodded again, and Dr. Rochmeier rose.

"There is nothing more I can do here," he declared. "Goodbye."

My mother extended her hand. "Thank you for coming, Dr. Rochmeier."

The doctor laughed. "Could I help it? You told me your husband was dying, you remember?"

"I remember," Mama said, "Anyway you forgave me. But it *was* good of you to come, and I thank you." She paid the doctor his fee of one dollar and ten cents for the pills, and saw him to the door.

Two weeks later my father was up and sitting in his rocking chair. A few weeks later he went back to work.

13

An Old-World Superstition Pursues Us to New York

WE HAD BEEN IN AMERICA nearly five years. It was the end of February 1912. Buried somewhere in those years were the hardships of our early struggles. I had passed my twelfth birthday and was very proud of the way I had mastered the English language, which I could speak without a trace of an accent. At least I thought I could. Anyway, Papa thought I spoke like a native. "It's a gift," he said. He himself managed quite well in English.

My mother? That was another story. Mama had a language all her own. She would Germanize her English in many ways, in accordance with her own feelings. "Liebchen," she would say to me, "Papa is coming schon heim. Geh 'runter mit dem pint." A pint was a tin can that actually held a quart and was used to carry home beer from the saloon. Or, she would say to a visitor, "Ach, es ist nice sie zu sehen."

Certainly America and my mother needed more time for each other. Six years and she could still feel weighed down by the burden of homesickness. My mother was in that state of divided feelings that plagued many immigrants. For her, the mail from "home" was easily the most important event of the day. About seven-thirty in the morning we would hear a shrill, warbling whistle from the bottom of the stairwell. It was like a policemen's whistle. The mailman blew it to announce the arrival of the first mail. "The letter man is here," Mama would say. And my father would go down to get the mail. News from home, some small family gossip to discuss at breakfast. Mama's sister had a new young man. Papa's second cousin, Irma, had married a brilliant young student who was coming to America. His new wife would follow later. Papa said he was not surprised, and my mother wiped away a tear.

After my father left for his job, Mama would settle down with another cup of coffee and read the mail once more with moist eyes. If there was mail for her, she would walk over to the sideboard in the front room and place her letter gently in its envelope and lay it away in the secret drawer in the dresser, which was locked. Her nest-egg gift from her father was also in that drawer. After that, Mama would wipe her eyes and I would start for school. When I came home for lunch, Mama was usually her normal self. Her depressions never lasted long. She would cry a little, dry her eyes, blow her nose, square her shoulders, and go on with the business of the day.

My mother was a fatalist. She believed there was a master plan for everyone, preordained at birth. She had the kind of mind that could accept the unusual and mysterious without questioning. "There is so much in this world that is yet to be understood," she would say. The unknown intrigued her. She was more religious than my father.

A strange experience occurred deep in the winter of 1912, for which we never found an explanation.

It was a bitter cold night. The window was tightly shut against the icy blasts. I was lying in my makeshift bed beside the window in the front room. There was a full moon. The room was light enough to outline everything. Then, suddenly, for some reason I woke up. I had the distinct feeling that I'd heard a sharp sound of breaking glass. Then again, that sharp crack. Then a third glass cracked. No splinters, just three wine glasses, standing on their shelf on the sideboard, cracked but unbroken.

Frightened now, I called out, staring with wide open eyes at the glasses. I called out again, and my mother, drawing a robe around her, came to my bed. "What is it, then?" she asked. I pointed to the sideboard. Then a fourth glass, with a fine ping, cracked. My mother was stunned. "Four glasses cracked," I said. She went to the cabinet and stood there for an instant.

"Somebody died," she said in a very low voice. "Please don't say that, Mama," I cried. "Yes," she reiterated, still in that low voice, "this is a sign that someone in the family has died." When my father joined us, they looked at the glasses. "Don't, you will break it," my mother said, when Papa reached out. They were extremely thin, expensive glasses my mother had brought with her from her more affluent European days. "I tell you," Mama insisted, "this is a sign. Someone near us has died." My father said this was nonsense. "No," Mama cried, "four glasses don't crack without reason, while we are sleeping."

"Nonsense," said my father again. "Come to bed, now, in the morning we will see what happened." He turned the gas down. "Go to sleep," he said to me. But for a long time I lay there, thinking. Could it be true, what Mama had said? I wondered. It was certainly weird, those glasses cracking. I could see that my parents had gone to the kitchen. The strong smell of brewing coffee wafted toward me. For some time there was silence. Then I heard Papa, "Put that foolishness out of our mind. In the morning we will find the explanation."

"No," Mama said, "You will find no reason for this. The explanation lies beyond our knowledge." Then she added, "It is the same as your miracles."

"What miracles?" asked my father.

"Those 'something will happen' miracles," said Mama.

Papa was silent. Then he said, "That is ridiculous. You know that *that* is only a saying. You know that." Papa laughed, "I assure you the gods have more important things to do than to single me out for their good deeds, and for that matter, neither do they give you advance notice of—of—things."

"I cannot answer this," Mama said. "But you'll see," she insisted. "We will get word, I know," she said in a sobbing voice, "These things happened in our family at home."

Now Papa asked, "What things?" After a while Mama said, "It happened when my mother's father died. I was about fifteen then. We were at dinner. All at once there was a crash in the bedroom. A huge, heavy mirror had fallen to the ground. You can understand that we were filled with shock. We stood staring at the thousand splinters lying on the carpet. And when my father looked for the hook that had been holding the mirror, he saw to his dismay that the hook was still in the wall."

"I must admit that—" Papa began.

"But wait," Mama cut in. "A few days later a messenger brought the news—my grandfather had died."

"A coincidence," said my father. "And you are being very foolish to believe otherwise."

"But the hook not coming down with the looking glass, is that coincidence? Is that normal?"

Papa did not reply immediately. "Well, answer me—is it normal?" Mama cried.

"How can I answer such a question?" Papa said. "How do I know what is normal? But I do know that there is a good, sound explanation for all this."

"But how did the glasses crack, just standing there, and all of us sleeping?" Mama argued. "And that mirror—?"

"That's ridiculous!" Papa cried.

"There you see, you are now angry, because you have

no answer."

"Good God!" Papa cried, "How do I know what caused that mirror to fall? Maybe it jumped off the hook. And furthermore, I'm going to bed."

"But those glasses," Mama called after him.

"I don't know, damn it." Now Papa was really angry. "And I don't care if all the spirits in Heaven are at work at this very moment, here in this house, cracking all the glasses—I'm going to sleep. Good night!"

I had the feeling that Papa was not at all the skeptic he professed. He was as shaken by this experience as my mother. This is what angered him when she probed too much.

My mother cleared away the cups. Papa said nothing after this. But for me it was all very exciting. Now their voices reached me more faintly. They had retired to the bedroom, but I could hear talk of Hungary and the strange things that occurred there from time to time. "Peasant talk," Papa said. "No, these things do happen," my mother insisted. "There are mysterious powers." She knew. She had a feeling that someone had died.

I must have fallen asleep. In the morning, when I awakened, Papa was standing beside the sideboard, examining the glasses. Not a splinter lying on the shelf. A small magnifying glass showed clear, sharp cracks. No one said anything. Papa just stood there rubbing his chin reflectively. Then he asked for a box. My mother was silently weeping. When I got back with a box whose contents I had emptied on the kitchen table, Papa took the glasses off the shelf. Then he packed them away in the box. He handled them very gently, with great care. Mama put the box on the top shelf in the closet. In the following days we tried to act as if nothing had happened. My father went down for the mail and then to work. Mama sat down with her second cup of coffee in the morning while I got ready for school. The usual routine. No one mentioned the glasses. It was an experience that we could not understand, and was best forgotten.

The days passed. One morning, when the mailman blew his whistle, my father went down to get the first mail. Mama served breakfast, eagerly awaiting the news from home. But that morning he was slow in coming back up. Something kept him downstairs.

"What is keeping your father?" Mama said to me, not really expecting an answer. "The letter man probably has more mail than usual," she said, half to herself, tapping the table with irritated fingers. "Papa will be late for his work—go down, Liebchen." But Papa was already opening the door. When he came in, his face was as white as a sheet. He was staring at a black-framed letter in his hand.

"No! Dear God, no!" my mother cried, and fainted.

When she came to, she learned that her sister Marisch had died. It had been a bad throat infection, Grandfather had written. And two days later that golden young life had been laid to rest, he had added. My aunt was twenty-two years old when she died.

My mother's sister Marisch. An old superstition
was confirmed by her sudden death at 22.

The letter was dated three days after the glasses cracked.

A coincidence? Perhaps.

My mother went about her work that day with tight lips and a frozen face. When Papa came home, supper was served and then Mama asked to be excused, and would Papa wash the dishes. He did, I dried and cleared up. Suddenly we heard Mama crying heavy, deep sobs, as if she would never stop. It was an awful thing to hear. My mother, would she never be consoled? It was my first experience with unbearable grief.

The next morning brought my mother to the kitchen, dressed and preparing breakfast. She said she felt better. She finished her coffee, even smiled a little, and went down to do the day's marketing.

All day she went around dry-eyed, but suddenly, with the awful reality of her sister's death, another crying spell brought my mother to her bed.

That went on day after day. There were quiet periods, then sudden sobbing spells. Then, one morning Mama said something very strange. She said that she would not cry anymore because her sister had scolded her severely. She remembered her dream clearly. "Leave me alone!" her sister had cried. "Let me go already," she had shouted angrily.

My father said nothing to this.

"You are not supposed to disturb the dead with your tears and lamentations," Mama told us. "It is written," she said. "I will let my sister rest."

14

When You Were Poor,
You Were a Democrat

O N   A   F I N E, balmy day in October 1912—one of those marvelous Indian summer days that bless New York occasionally before the chill winds and winter snows set in—Papa became a citizen of the United States.

For us it was a day to remember.

Our immigrant days were over. Suddenly we were part and parcel of the American scene. We had been thinking about it for years, imagining how wonderful it had to be when one no longer felt a stranger in a strange country.

Papa lost no time in declaring himself a Democrat, completely enamored of Woodrow Wilson, the "Herr Professor," to the immense satisfaction of Mr. Resch, our landlord, who was also the captain of our precinct. Joseph Resch had a great interest in fostering Democratic principles in the people who lived in his building. What those principles were, no one really understood, except that when we were poor, you were a Democrat, and you went to Mr. Resch, who fixed things when you were in trouble.

In his late fifties, Mr. Resch was a tall, heavyset man with great, powerful shoulders. He was probably the only politician the people we knew ever came into direct contact with. As a result, he had a tremendous impact upon everyone. And why not? Here he was, an immigrant like ourselves. He had arrived from Germany in the eighties. He was a precinct captain, with his eyes on any political plums Tammany Hall offered on the bargain counter; and he was rich. At least he was rich by our standards. He owned the building we lived in; the beer saloon in our building belonged to him; the building next door was his, too.

And now my father was a citizen. Mama immediately looked to Mr. Resch to "*do* something for my husband." It was incumbent upon the highly placed Democrat to help his new citizen into a political job that might bring the better life which had so far eluded her.

But Papa would have none of it, "I have a good job," he said.

Papa's idea of a good job and my mother's idea of a good job differed considerably. He earned fifteen dollars a week. He had gotten a dollar raise not too long before. Occasionally he worked later when a shipment required special attention. Another dollar.

"You should better yourself now that you are a citizen," Mama suggested, heatedly. It was a hopeless cause. My father was not a man in whom the juices of ambition stirred too violently. He lived with a quiet contentment. And he hated change. When he left in the morning at seven-thirty, he knew he was going to a job he liked, he knew what was expected of him, and he knew that he was good at that job. The prospect of working with the unfamiliar floored Papa completely.

So now Papa was a citizen. Some weeks later, at election time, dressing carefully so that he might go to the polls in style, Papa cast his first ballot. That night, Mr. Resch organized his customary Election Day block party and torchlight parade. An unforgettable sight, to see the marchers slowly making headway through the streets, Mr. Resch's figure towering above the others, the flaming torches held high above heads, lighting the sky. It was an exciting thing to see those bobbing flames, flickering like fireflies in the dark of night.

Just as the celebration was starting, I was marched upstairs, but I was allowed to spend the evening on the fire-escape, watching. People were milling about, their faces beaming, and in the moonlight, I could see my father standing with a group, waving his arms energetically, probably discussing the political scene he had just become part of.

Now the party was in full swing. The German band started a lively polka, and people began pairing off. There were kegs of beer near two tables piled with sandwiches from the free lunch counter in Mr. Resch's saloon.

Toward midnight, the musicians closed up shop. One of them made the rounds, hat in hand, to collect their reward for their contribution towards the evening's festivities. People began looking at their watches. Suddenly the reality of the following day's work brought the party to an end, and with slow steps, they began moving away.

A small group of my parents' closest friends gathered in our kitchen for one last toast, beer glasses held high, one last "Prosit" sung before they, too, made their way home.

Now it was two o'clock in the morning. My parents were in their room, and I was lying on my makeshift bed in the front room, looking out at the stars and wishing that nothing would ever change, not ever, from the way things were then.

15

Buy Now, Pay Later—
Mama Discovers an American Custom

OUT OF THE BITS AND PIECES of my early immigrant memories, I remember the time when my
mother became acquainted with the experience of making purchases "without the money to pay right away,"
as she put it.

After we moved next door, into the flat vacated by
the Walshes, Mama discovered that with moving unexpected expenses would crop up. First came the discovery
that the linoleum on the kitchen floor required replac-
ing. Then Mama discovered the unhappy fact that her
new front room had two windows. Curtains were needed for that second window. She had not paid too much
attention to the Walsh's windows when she visited
there. "Here is another window." Mama's face clouded.
"How could I have forgotten that the Walshes had two
windows in the front room? Where will I find the money
for curtains?"

Another calamity stared mother in the face when she
tried to place the furniture that was transferred from the
rooms next door. Suddenly everything seemed to have

147

changed shape. Any semblance to the furniture we had lived with these years was gone, and defects she never noticed suddenly became apparent. The sofa, the very same one that my father had bought for our first home, suddenly decided to show its age.

"My God, so many things to buy—so little money," she sighed.

So, now my mother was faced with the dilemma of whether or not to dig into the "nest egg", that sum of money she had received from her father so many years before. Later, when I grew up, I learned that Grandfather's gift had been about a thousand kroner—one hundred dollars. Not bad, for those days. My mother was so emotionally bound to that money that it became a tug of war between her aesthetic values and her feelings. Did she really need these new curtains, linoleum, furniture?

In the end, she decided that she did. That proverbial rainy day could no longer be put off. She would use her nest egg. A difficult decision.

Well, it turned out that she did not have to use her money after all. Her friend, Mrs. Wagner, came to the rescue. Mrs. Wagner lived in the flat over us. She was a German lady who came to this country about the time we did. She was alone. Her husband had taken off for parts unknown, soon after they landed. After that, the unhappy lady decided to share her home with two ladies, 'to help pay the rent,' as did most of the tenants in the building. My mother and Mrs. Wagner were good friends, happily speaking German when they were together.

During the course of one visit, my mother unburdened herself of the dilemma that faced her.

"Just look at this room," she cried, waving her arm. "Nothing is the right size; either too small or too big. Nothing looks right here. And just look at that sofa—it is a complete surprise to me how worn out and shapeless everything is. All of a sudden I see defects I never noticed before."

Mrs. Wagner nodded sympathetically. It was obvious that the furniture, transferred from the old place, could not be accommodated in their new surroundings. The perfectly acceptable had become impossible within new walls. For my mother it was a shattering experience.

She turned to her friend. "I thought already that maybe I would not pay the rent for two months. Thirty dollars—it would help."

Mrs. Wagner looked uncertain. "Well, I don't know—"

"Now that Papa is a citizen—I mean, I could speak to Resch." Mr. Resch was our landlord. He was also the local politician. He was supposed to help people, especially citizens.

"Kill me he won't. Every month he comes to the door for the rent. Every month I have the rent in the sugar bowl. I think once, as citizens, we can ask him to wait for the money."

Paying rent rated first in my mother's book of unhappy experiences.

"Another month passed already?" she would cry. Every February she argued for a reduction, considering how short the month was. A yearly hassle.

Mama turned to her friend. "Do you think thirty dollars—no, I can add five—thirty-five, I think would buy what I need. Curtains, linoleum, maybe a new sofa and a chair."

Mrs. Wagner looked at Mama. She was about to say something, but thought better of it. Mama caught it. "You were going to say?"

"Well, I don't know. Thirty-five dollars would not buy too much. Everything is so expensive these days.

Mama shook her head and sighed. "Maybe curtains —and the linoleum must be changed—and maybe a new sofa."

"Why don't you buy everything the way I do?" suggested the lady.

"I don't know what you mean—how do you buy things?"

"A man comes to my door and sells things. I pay a little the first time and then I pay a little every week."

"And you buy furniture this way? And curtains?"

"Yes, of course," Mrs. Wagner laughed. "I buy everything this way. Ten cents a week, I pay for small things. Furniture is fifty cents.

"But this is wonderful, absolutely wonderful. For furniture, how much is there to pay the first time?" My mother's practical side came to the forefront. "You said he sells furniture too."

150

"Yes, he has connections. I imagine five—maybe ten dollars at first will buy everything you need. The whole house buys from him. I'm surprised he never came to your door."

"Maybe he did—I don't remember. But I never knew that you can buy furniture without having the money to pay right away. So many come to the door to sell things, but no one ever told me about that fifty cents a week for furniture. I would have remembered *that*. I had no idea!"

"I'm surprised. Finkleman is usually selling here on Friday. Every Friday he knocks on the doors and sells something. Even jewelry."

"Jewelry even!" Mama shook her head. "My God, even jewelry!" She added gaily. "Maybe I will buy a big diamond—would Papa open *his* eyes."

Mrs. Wagner laughed. "And don't forget the curtains —ten cents a week."

She arose from her chair and my mother got up with her.

"I will send Finkleman down to see you when he comes next week to collect," said the lady. "And thank you for the coffee. The cake was delicious."

"Oh, it was nothing—a pleasure. I think I should thank you, my dear, dear friend. You have saved my life."

"Oh, I'm sure it was not as bad as all that," laughed the lady.

"Well, maybe I made more of it that I should have.

151

But you must agree that this room and my old things just don't go together."

"Well, Finkleman will fix it for you. And now I must go."

"You will send Finkleman to see me?"

"Yes, of course, don't worry."

Well, my mother was not exactly worried. But it seemed too good to be true. That her problem was going to be solved without her touching her nest egg, she could not believe. And that the rent postponement plan could be dropped, was more than a relief. No, Mama was not worried, but it put her on edge to wait.

Another fine American custom to be marvelled at. A person can buy things without having to pay immediately. "Only in America," she said to Papa in the evening. "Where else can a poor man have a life? For ten cents a week you buy sheets, for fifty cents—"

"What ten cents—what fifty cents?" Papa interrupted, alarmed.

"Nothing," said Mama. "I was just saying how wonderful it is here for people."

For some reason my father did not follow this up as I had expected. Then he said, suppressing a yawn, "And this ends another day in our new home."

It had been a long day for him. He had worked late. It was after nine when he got home.

All that following day, it was Sunday, Mama walked about with a faraway look, as if she were not on the same planet with us. Then suddenly she would take pencil and paper and sit lost in thought. It almost seemed that now, with the means at hand to furnish her new front room, she was suddenly thrown off course. Actually, it was no small thing to combine her heart's desire with her naturally practical and prudent nature.

On Monday morning Finkleman came. He spread his wares on the couch and the table with the flourish of a loving father. His technique must have been persuasive. When he left Mama had not only purchased curtains and linoleum, but a set of dishes decorated with garlands of daisies. "For everyday use," Mama explained.

Frank Trotta, the iceman, helped lay the linoleum on the kitchen floor. My father was all thumbs when it came to such intricate labors as cutting spaces around sinks and stoves. Mama paid Frank fifty cents. She cut a slice of cake for him to take home, with the admonishment, "to come tomorrow early."

"Missus, don't worry, I will be here right after the mister goes to work."

The next day he came with his cart to take the front room furniture away. In exchange he gave us free ice deliveries for the summer. Three months' worth of ice for our front-room furniture seemed like a lopsided bargain, but this time my mother was in no mood to take her advantage.

I can still remember the uproar when my father came home to face this, another of my mother's 'brilliant ideas', as he called them. Papa did not like change.

Mama thrived on it, when it gave a distinct advantage.

When the key grated in the door that day, Mama sat down to await the blast she knew was coming. She didn't have long to wait.

"Verdammt! What is going on here? Where is everything? *Where is it*?" Papa waved a frantic arm. "What have you done with my CHAIR?"

"What chair?" Mama asked innocently.

"What chair, you ask? MY CHAIR! MY CHAIR!" My father shouted.

And Mama came straight out with it, when Papa said, "Stop playing games. Where is my chair, where is everything?" he added, suddenly realizing that, in fact, everything was missing.

"I sold the front room to Frank," she said simply. "You saw yourself how worn and out of shape everything was."

"But my chair—you should have asked me."

"Would you have agreed?"

Papa laughed then. "Probably not.   But you should have asked anyway," he added.

"I know," said Mama. "I'm sorry."

"Well, what's done is done. What you do with your money is actually your affair. But, if you don't mind, I will have my chair back."

"But, I bought another rocking chair—a nice, upholstered—"

"Return it—I will not sacrifice my chair for your fancy parlor," Papa said, walking toward the door.

"Will Papa get his chair back?" I asked my mother.

"I don't think he will get it back," Mama said slowly. "I think Frank had a customer before he took our things away," she added with a little smile.

Then I asked, "Why didn't you tell Papa about the ten-cents and the fifty-cents-a-week arrangements? He thinks you—"

"I will tell him in time. When Papa needs a new suit—I will tell him."

When I graduated, Papa needed a new suit. That is when he learned of the installment arrangements with the peddler Finkleman. I wondered why no one called him Mr. Finkleman. It was only Finkleman. If he had a first name no one asked.

"So you found a way not to touch your money," Papa asked, smiling.

It occurs to me that my father was actually quite impressed with this new way of acquiring things. Probably because bank accounts remained intact. Without a bank account, the uncertainties of life remained too unbearable.

Papa's rocker was sold before he got to Frank. As Mama had said, it had already been spoken for. The new chair, sitting beside the wall, under the window, soon became "my chair" for Papa.

16

How Papa Learned
About Women's Rights

BY AND LARGE, my early years were happy years. As each day ended, we knew what the next day would bring. When my father left the house in the morning we knew that he was going to his job. When I came home after school, I knew Mama would be waiting with milk and thin slices of buttered bread. Sundays, Papa played pinochle with friends; neighbors would come calling and talk of the old days and their life in the new country. On Monday the wheels of our existence started their same full turn. Life was uncomplicated and simple. I can honestly say that we were happy. I suppose we just managed to be happy with what we had.

Of the few unhappy memories, perhaps the most unpleasant was the time my father lost the job he had held for eight years. That was in 1915. The firm he worked for had a new manager who introduced changes which affected some employees, my father among them. There came the day that he was replaced. It was regretted, but the new personnel manager considered the change necessary. No reason given.

HOW PAPA LEARNED ABOUT WOMEN'S RIGHTS

In the meantime, something had to be done. Expenses continued—with nothing coming in. Mama decided to go out and do day work, as some women in the building did, but Papa wouldn't hear of such a thing. "Something will happen, something always happens, you'll see," he said, as usual, to comfort Mama.

For an answer, Mama only humphed.

"All right, worry if it pleases you. But you will not go out to work. It is my job to provide. Your job is in the home."

"That's fine—very fine—but what will we use for money—your pinochle beans?"

"Oh, pardon me," my father said, "This I had not thought of."

The next day Papa came home with the announcement that our worries were over. He was going to start a French laundry business, "at home, here in the kitchen."

My mother stood there for a while as if she had not heard what he had said. Then she laughed, "My dear husband, you are insane. A French laundry? What in heaven's name is a French laundry?"

"My French laundry," Papa explained, "will launder only fine, delicately embroidered wearables of the rich. The charges will be according to the value of the articles washed and ironed." My mother shook her head in amazement. "But where will you find such rich people? Not in this neighborhood!"

"Of course not. I have already placed advertisements in three American papers, and the *StaatsZeitung*. Many

157

rich people read the German paper," he added.

Papa needed twenty dollars for a down payment on a washing machine, steam iron, various soaps, bleaches and blueing. Handicapped by memories of former business tragedies, he had a most difficult time selling her this new idea.

Well, finally my father managed to talk Mama into making him a small loan from her nest egg. "But my kitchen I will not give up," Mama warned. "Only a corner," answered Papa, "behind the door. Just enough space for the machine."

That washing machine was something to behold. After a batch of laundry was finished, one could not help wondering whether the whole thing would not have been as easy the old way with a washboard. Since the machine was not run by electricity, Papa had to push a hand lever back and forth, back and forth—a most tiring effort, he had to admit. Still my father consoled himself with the time the machine saved, when his muscles screamed with the pain of the unaccustomed effort.

There were no sheets or flat things accepted. Occasionally, an embroidered pillow case or a lace tablecloth found its way into Papa's favor. Mama agreed to do the fancy ironing.

It was becoming a flourishing business.

Without realizing it, Mama became more and more involved. Gradually there came a change in the normal routine of our lives. I helped with the cooking and baking, but the wonderful apricot nut tarts disappeared from our table. Only Mama could turn out those delicate, mouthwatering morsels.

At last, Papa's ideas were paying off. But there was a price for our much improved financial circumstances. My father became obsessed with his business. For the first time, he was tasting the heady juice of business success, and it did something to him. He could not separate himself from his business. He had eyes and ears only for his new venture. Books were laid aside. The card games ceased. We no longer visited museums on Sunday afternoons. More and more packages of laundry accumulated. The kitchen shrank with all that activity. Slowly, Papa's fine, considerate character changed. He became tense, irritable, unnatural. The trick of giving orders now came easily.

One day, something in Mama snapped. We were finishing our supper. Papa brought out a half a dozen embroidered napkins for Mama to iron. They were the last of a package Papa was to deliver in the morning to a rich customer on Seventy-second Street and Riverside Drive. I started to clear the table when suddenly Mama went to the ironing board, closed it, and calmly put it away in the closet, where it had not rested since business began; and then she walked out. From the front room she cried, "I will not iron for you another thing in the evening—not today—not any other day. You have become impossible!"

My mother had had enough, and she was angry, really angry. But some time elapsed before my father understood how angry she *really* was.

There were loud words that evening. Niether could understand the changed attitude of the other. Minor infractions became major irritations. Without giving it much thought, Papa had accepted more work than he could handle. The pressures had mounted with longer and longer ironing shifts and with my mother grimly working into the night—without recognition. That is what irked her most and brought on the first flareup. My mother's nature rebelled against being taken for granted.

In the end, Papa agreed to limit his business to the customers he now had, with no work on Sunday. But the bug had bitten my father; he could not get himself to refuse new business when it came his way.

"Just this fine silk blouse," Papa pleaded. "I promised delivery in the morning. Only the blouse."

"No," Mama flatly refused. "I will not iron another thing for you in the evening." She stood there, small and angry and determined. "I have found work in the bakery. Two hours in the evening. For this I will get paid at least, and a thank you once in a while. From you what do I get? Nothing. Iron the blouse yourself. Supper will be on the table six o'clock. Seven I go to the bakery."

This infuriated my father. "I forbid it—"

Mama shouted back, "You forbid it! You can no longer forbid anything. You have your laundry—"

HOW PAPA LEARNED ABOUT WOMEN'S RIGHTS

"My laundry! MY LAUNDRY! I am doing this for myself?"

Mama said he was—and on and on the argument went. Papa stormed out of the house. When he returned, he said that he was moving the laundry into the basement. Now, I thought, there will be peace. Mama will not be angry any more. But I might have known; my mother was not an easy forgiver. She did not say one word at supper that evening. And from then on, she kept her distance.

Mrs. Morris, the janitress, was now employed to do all the ironing. About ten in the morning, after her janitorial work was done, she came to the corner in the basement where Papa had set up his quarters. Not once did Mama come down to the basement to see how things were getting on. She changed her mind about going out to work in the bakery. She found embroidery homework. This gave more time for the house. She sat with the embroidery; then she went into contracting; she herself now distributed work among some of her friends.

To be sure, she had her kitchen to herself once more, but there was no change; she continued to be angry with Papa. His autocratic ways still rankled.

A curious double life now existed with Papa's basement work. My father remained in his makeshift laundry all hours of the day, never coming up till late at night, tired and silent. Silently, too, Mama heated his supper, then went back to their room. My father opened

161

a bed for himself in the kitchen.

In this way week after week went by without a change in their attitudes. And then my mother took to her bed for a few days with a cold. And I caught her wiping her eyes when I came in. Once my father came away from the basement to ask how she was, and for an instant I thought he was going toward the bedroom, but then he turned abruptly and walked away. Now I was certain that both were unhappy with the way things were, though neither would admit it.

After my mother recovered, I went down to see how things were getting on there, and if my father needed my help. No, Mrs. Morris was doing well but would I stay a while? Before I knew it, his troubled soul poured out his unhappiness. He hated calling for and delivering the finished product. He hated using servants' elevators. I realized suddenly, as he talked that he would like nothing better than to go back to the old tranquil life, to a job; a nice, respectable job, with respectable hours.

But he continued, with a furious determination, to call for the wash and deliver it.

One day my father came up earlier than usual. We were having our supper, and when my mother moved to get up he motioned to her to remain seated. Caught by surprise, she remained in her chair and then suddenly she began to cry, in loud, convulsive sobs. Papa got up to comfort her. And then, in an improbable moment, Papa admitted he'd had enough; enough of the laundry, enough of this breach in the family. He was going back to work. Financially he was in good shape. The laundry had made money. He had all of it banked, with the exception of that weekly money he had given Mama. I could see he was rather pleased with himself; and I was glad for him. Papa decided to go and look for a job again.

Well, events swiftly brought Papa's gods into play. Miraculously, at just that time his old firm wrote and invited him back provided he was listed as "Hermann" on the books. It seems there was a policy against hiring employees with certain names. My father had no objections.

In one week Papa delivered the last of the laundry, paid Mrs. Morris, and closed his business. The French laundry game had lasted eight months.

17

Great Changes

IT WAS 1917.

With the flow of the passing years, great changes had come about in our lives—pictures that moved, machines that reached the skies, horseless carriages, and bulbs that illuminated our homes in place of gas lamps.

Meanwhile, the early immigrant had grown with these changes. He had achieved, in some measure, the fulfillment of his dreams and aspirations. In a way, he had reached the end of his road. He had done his job.

But missing was so much that gave his early life its flavor, so much that was fine and deep. An end had come to the warm friendliness he had known. The ferment of his dreams was gone, the great American romance was gone; something within himself had gone with it. It would never be again—the fullness and richness and stirring adventure that had brought him to this land when it was young.

Oh, there had been times when his spirit came near to breaking, when his courage faltered, but he had stayed with the struggle, and had taken the bad with the good.

No, it had not been easy; it had not been a great life always. But difficult and demanding as life was, in retrospect there emerges a grandeur from it all.

It had been a simple life, with simple pleasures, with good people. Among our most pleasurable diversions was the street musician. When one of those colorful singers came to our street, windows were raised and people, leaning on their elbows, looked down, enjoying the songs that swept upwards. A recollection brings to mind one young singer who visited our street regularly. He was very young, no more than twenty. He was handsome, with fine, dark eyes that would look up to his audience with a smile in them. His face was framed by brown curls that showed longer down his back than was the custom of the day. He wore his hat turned up on one side at a rakish angle. A faded, velvet jacket that had been brown once, with a red scarf flowing freely in the breeze, completed the costume.

When the voice of the flamboyant young singer floated upwards towards our kitchen, my mother would drop everything and go to the window where she stood moist-eyed listening to her favorite song. At first he sang it accidentally, but when she asked him the next time he came to our street to sing it again he made a deep bow and courteously obliged.

"Du, du, liegst mir im Herzen,
Du, du, liegst mir im Sinn,
Du, du, machst mir viel Schmerzen,
Weisst nicht wie gut ich dier bin."

165

How often have I heard my mother quietly humming this song from her old-country memories.

After the young singer had finished his song, he would thank his audience with a deep bow and a wide sweep of his hat, before gathering the coins that had been wrapped in paper and tossed down from the windows.

A little later we could hear a faint echo of his next performance fading away in the distance.

How I remember those street scenes, how they crop up in the memory of my childhood. There was the German Band which came to our street regularly, and to which we little girls danced. Foolish, little tripping dances they were. First on one leg, twirling the other one around and around to the rhythm of the music. Then, a change to the other leg, when the whole process was repeated, performing the same childish acrobatic stunts.

And of course the organ grinder and his tiny companion, the monkey wearing his red fez, who mischieviously cavorted about among the people from whom he collected the pennies for his master. Surely he managed to get a chuckle or two from those who watched him. But he, too, has disappeared from the streets of New York.

Now, looking back to these street entertainments, I smile a little as I recall the enjoyable role they played in our lives.

But the dark shadow of war had come to Europe.

The organ grinder.

Already the terrible epitaph of the old world was being written in the blood of its young men. And eventually, in April 1917, the United States declared war on the Central Powers.

Our immigrant days were over. Papa did not buy the *StaatsZeitung* any more.

There were days of anguish and grief. And then it ended, the war for democracy. On November eleventh of the following year, 1918, the fighting was over.

And gradually the country went back to normal.

Still, after the first World War, nothing was the same again.

All Europe had become impoverished with that war. And people, in desperation, saw in America their only hope. They came in droves, abandoning their homeland with its grim history of death and starvation.

But postwar America was in no mood for these strangers, in whom it saw a danger and a threat to its own welfare.

The United States, fearful of being overrun by the multitudes from the war-torn lands, passed restrictive laws. And in 1924, with the new quota system in effect, America closed its gates that had been open to the world.

A trickle of immigrants passed through Ellis Island after that.

An era had ended.

Perhaps it had to end, this vast migration of people; perhaps it had gotten to be too much. I don't know. I do know that without that great surge of humanity, whose initiative and courage carried them here, America would not be what it is today. The tremendous storehouse of brainpower, vitality and strength in those teeming millions is ours only because of the free flow of the immigrants who braved the ocean to seek their opportunity in the new land.

And if I see this era with romantic eyes, it is because it *was* a romantic era. Who can deny the romance of a world flocking by the millions to the lure of the phenomenon called America?

And now, as I write this, an aging lady looking back down the years, it is my hope that I have touched, at least in part, the essence of that remarkable time when the shores of America were open to the world.

It was then, and will never be again.

In 1924
a quota
system went
into effect.
Gradually
the great Hall
on Ellis Island
grew silent.
*An era
had ended.*

Picture Credits

I am indebted to my son, Robert Jastrow, for collecting the photographs and illustrations relating to the great wave of immigration in the first decade of the century, and for the scenes of New York life during my childhood years. He was very ably supported in this research by Marjorie Ingle of Columbia University and Ann Novotny of Research Reports. The photographs on individual pages are reproduced by courtesy of the following individuals and institutions:

Page

48 *and* 49   Library of Congress, Prints and Photographs
                Division.
50 *and* 51   Museum of the City of New York, Byron
                Collection
52 *and* 53   National Parks Service, Augustus F. Sherman
                Collection
54 *and* 55   New York Public Library, Local History and
                Genealogy Division (William Williams Collection)
56   Library of Congress, Prints and Photographs
                Division
57   New York Public Library, Local History and
                Genealogy Division
58 *and* 59   Library of Congress, Prints and Photographs
                Division
60 *and* 61   Staten Island Historical Society, Alice Austen
                Collection